MAKING SENSE

A HANDBOOK FOR THE FUTURE OF WORK

EXPRESS EDITION

ON
OFF

LYNNE CAZALY

First published May 2015

1 2

Copyright © 2015 Lynne Cazaly

www.lynnecazaly.com

National Library of Australia Cataloguing-in-Publication entry:
Author: Lynne Cazaly, 1964 -
Title: Making Sense: A Handbook for the Future of Work
ISBN: 9780987462954

Subjects: Leadership.
                     Strategy.
                     Thinking.
                     Change.
                     Teams.
                     Future.
                     Innovation.
                     Creativity.
                     Collaboration.
                     Communication.

Illustrations and layout by Lynne Cazaly

Cover design by Lliam Amor

Research Assistance by Myra May Lahoylahoy

MAKING SENSE

A HANDBOOK FOR THE FUTURE OF WORK

EXPRESS EDITION

LYNNE CAZALY

Foreword

It can be entertaining to see how we predict the future. From characters like The Robot on *Lost in Space,* to any *Star Trek* episode, we are always imagining into the future and picturing what our world will be like. Reading Alvin Toffler's *Future Shock* or the classic from George Orwell *1984,* watching science fiction and thinking of future technology... we're predicting what it might be like up there, in the future.

Equally entertaining is when we then look back and see where we've come from; there may have been plug and cord switchboards for telephones or we hear the old dial up noises that connected us to the earliest versions of the Internet. Or when see an older film – not just from the 1940s or 50s but from the 1990s or early 2000s - and see the technology we used to use: big boxy mobile phones with external antennas and battery packs the size of suitcases? What were we thinking!?

Today we continue to use all that we know and all that we can get our hands and minds on to predict and plan for the future. How do we make sense of the **now** to plan for the **future**?

We are humans and we use sense making. We make our best guess. Our discussions, thinking and mapping help us predict and scope, ponder and plan.

And then we look back on it ... and sense is made... and often it's not quite as we thought is might be. We might smile or shake our heads and laugh at what we were thinking then. But it's what we knew at the time. We made sense of what we knew at the time. We proposed scenarios, situations, possibilities and options. We were creative and thought provoking and making our best guess of what the future would be like or what we could do based on what know now.

In the world of work today, for the future of work, we have to keep doing our best to make sense.

This is not a book *about* the future of work; it's a book that will help you *handle* the future of work... whatever it is, whatever happens, however it impacts you. This book is full of approaches, questions, techniques, tools and models to help you as you respond to what the future has in store- for you, your team, your organisation, industry, country... your world.

It is a tool and a handbook that will help you put your sense making to work. You see, this sense making topic has got some balls, and that's where it can get tricky. It's a capability needed in workplaces and communities today and the irony is that it can be difficult to make sense of making sense.

There's such a depth of information on the topic of sensemaking; journals, well-researched articles and peer reviewed detailed pieces that go deep, deep, deep on sensemaking. But I don't think they help us make sense of making sense. Time is of the essence. How do we make sense swiftly? How do we get smart... quick?

This is my thinking and experience on how I've worked with people, to help them work together to think, map and act... to make sense of whatever is going on in their industry, their organisation, their team... or for themselves.

It's a book that is about making sense. And no matter what the future holds, no matter what technology comes or what changes are made to the world we live in, we will always be striving to make sense of what's going on.

We are humans and we use sense making.
Making Sense: A Handbook for the Future of Work.

Lynne.

Contents

New times call for new decisions

Those critical choices you made then, they were based on what you knew about the world as it was.

But now, you know more and the world is different.

So why spend so much time defending those choices?

We don't re-decide very often, which means that most of our time is spent doing, not choosing. And if the world isn't changing (if you're not changing) that doing makes a lot of sense.

The pain comes from falling in love with your status quo and living in fear of making another choice, a choice that might not work.

You might have been right then, but now isn't then, it's now.
If the world isn't different, no need to make a new decision.

The only question, then, "is the world different now"?

- Seth Godin

Once upon a time

...a team worked for weeks on a pack of information.

The team. That's more than one person.
And weeks. That's more than a couple of hours one afternoon.

A team and weeks. Putting a pack of information together so that other people could make sense of what was going on with a project in an organisation.

The team hadn't worked with this information before. They needed to make sense of it before they shaped and shared it. (It's like how being a teacher of something makes you way more knowledgeable and way more clear about something. You've got to understand it well before you tell, teach or train someone else.)

So there they are... working away.

For weeks.

If you're making sense of this story you'll see it's about multiple people spending a lot of time. A quick calculation, five people, let's say at a minimum 20 hours a week (half their time in the office, the rest spent on less productive activities, lunch, breaks and meetings) and you have 100 hours a week on this pack.

Multiplied by weeks. Let's say, five. Five hundred hours trying to make sense of something and package it up so it can be shared and implemented, followed and used as a reference for future work on this project.

Five hundred hours, let's say they're earning $50 an hour. $25000 - whatever the currency - on trying to make sense of something, together.

How is the information coming together? Slowly. They're making progress, but slowly. They get a first or second draft going. Great work team!

Then the leader of the team spends a couple of hours 'smashing' it in to shape.

Great work again!

Then that draft is circulated around the team and... there is a halt to progress.

Oh look, a puppy! Let's head off on a tangent.

One of the team, let's call her Lisa, isn't happy. Doesn't say anything, just heads home at the end of the day and then starts work.

She starts work at midnight and pushes on through until 4am, creating a NEW pack of information.

What???!!!! A new pack!?

You mean she's not working on the existing one? Or even the first or second draft? She goes off, over there, in another direction, creating another freakin' pack of information.

Struggling to make sense of things so she can package it up in a way that works for her, she pretty much deletes and ignores the weeks and weeks of sense making effort of the team ... to have a crack at a whole new piece of sense.

Different version, edits and viewpoints are great; but I wonder...

Where is the sense?

Why didn't she say something?

Which parts of the first pack is she not comfortable with?

Why wasn't she asked?

Where's the checkpoint, the milestone and the 'wait a minute' moments where we stop to see if we are indeed making any sense?

Where is our sense check on how our sense making is going?

Making Sense - Lynne Cazaly

This is crazy! Yet this goes on in teams in businesses every day around the world.

It's counterproductive, time wasting, ambiguity creating and complexity making.

Too often we humans create our own complexity and ambiguity. It's human made. Just as the solution to sense making is human made, so too is the problem.

Until we see that <u>we</u> are creating the confusion, uncertainty and 'wtf is going on', we won't get to clarity quickly enough to meet the demands of the current and future way of the world.

It's got to stop.

Sense has to start.

There needs to be a daily dose, an hourly dose, and a minute-by-minute dose of sense making. And we shouldn't proceed until we've 'got it'.

Oh, and that pack of information Lisa and the leader and the team were grappling with? Sixty-eight pages of mind-numbing confusion, eight weeks later. It was like they wee saying 'dim the lights, drawn the shades, lock the door and make them listen to my damn PowerPoint'. Groan!

★ www.lynnecazaly.com

What is this thing called sensemaking?
Some call it sense making. See the space there?
Two words : sense and making.

I think of it as simply making sense.

It's how we structure the unknown
so we can make sense of it
and then get to work acting on it.

Why we need to make sense

"Long-term decisions start in the short term, so understanding how the world is changing in real time is far more valuable immediately than trying to guess what will happen in the world 20 years from now."

From 'Non-Obvious: How to Think Different, Curate Ideas &
Predict The Future'

- Rohit Bhargava

Making Sense - Lynne Cazaly

Why make sense

It's pretty scary out there. There is this VUCA thing. Volatility, uncertainty, complexity and ambiguity. And here are some charts, continuums and high tech visual graphs about VUCA and why it makes sense to make sense.

VOLATILITY INDEX ✱ www.lynnecazaly.com

Volatility… it's when you just don't know what's coming next. Think shifting sands in the desert. One day it looks like this, the next day it's a different landscape. It may be tricky to understand and damn it, it keeps changing.

People are volatile and so are events, circumstances, environments, systems and processes. Combine them all and you have some potentially explosive situations.

The main volatility today is how organizations, systems and structures change. There is upheaval, constantly.

And the volatility isn't slowing down anytime soon. The Global Volatility Index is off the charts and it starts to make us feel a bit 'aaarrrggghhhh'.

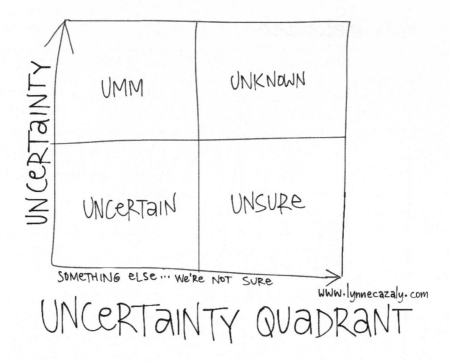

UNCERTAINTY QUADRANT

Uncertainty... It's when there's ummm. Despite business modeling, futurist thinking, projections and extrapolations, we still aren't totally certain what's ahead, what will happen next and what it means for us.

For many, job security is uncertain and the impact of restructures and re-organisations creates uncertainty. It's an uneasy feeling not knowing.

It's like when you're waiting for results from a medical test. There's this 'no man's land' between having the tests and waiting to hear. One way or the other. This or that. Or some other thing. It's unsettling, disruptive and the mind goes wandering and wondering what could be.

Uncertainty feels disruptive. It stops us taking risks, contributing greatness and doing good work. We hesitate, pause, freeze and hover in analysis paralysis.

Making Sense - Lynne Cazaly

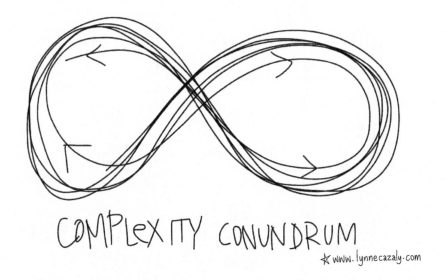

COMPLEXITY CONUNDRUM

*www.lynnecazaly.com

Complexity stems from four main areas:

Us. You. Me. Them

That's it. We humans are contributing to higher levels of complexity than ever before.

Structures keep changing, new products and services keep hitting the shelves and businesses change the way they're doing things. New versions are released, updated programs are issued and rather than making things easier or sharper, they throw us into another loop of having to relearn, make sense and get even more of a grip than we thought we had.

It's a little like the GPS system on your smart phone, tablet or in your vehicle. It will find you the shortest, quickest, most direct route... or you can take the longer, scenic route.

Watch out for the scenic route in work; sometimes it sets off an infinity loop or complexity conundrum and you'll never know where it will end or where it started.

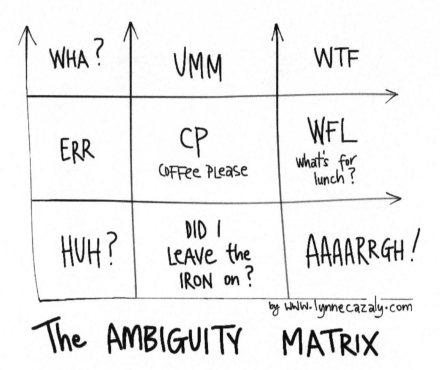

The AMBIGUITY MATRIX

by www.lynnecazaly.com

Ambiguity is when you don't know what is impacting or affecting what. What do you do? What plan do you follow? What do you do next… and then what after that?

So many questions. Ambiguity is often revealed as indecision, uncertainty in big doses and vague outcomes. Think non-committal. And then comes inaction.

If we don't know what we're doing, then we don't do much. And then we don't know what we're doing with what we are doing… so we don't do much more.

Ok so my visual models of volatility, uncertainty, complexity and ambiguity may be my humorous way of looking at VUCA … but the impacts of VUCA are real and ongoing. VUCA isn't going away anytime soon. We've got to make sense of what's going on and then respond.

Making Sense - Lynne Cazaly

The Need for Sense

In writing this book, what follows here are some of the discussions, rants and topics that cropped up in conversation with colleagues, clients and customers. What do you think...?

So the world is VUCA ...
The world is VUCA - volatility, uncertainty, complexity and ambiguity. And it's not slowing down anytime soon. In fact it's getting more volatile, complex, uncertain and ambiguous. Some of it we control, other parts we create.

... and we're working with people
We're just humans living with other humans. We work with them, speak with them, problem solve with them and create wondrous things with them. I think too often we forget we're working with humans. We get so used to looking at the screen in our hand, the screen on our desk and the big screen on the wall at home that we forget how to think, listen and deliver sensical information to other humans.

Information is dense
The information we read, work with and need to digest is thick, dense and detailed. We wade waist-deep through it. While many people work in the field of knowledge work creating and crafting information, we still need to sort through what we want and avoid what we don't. That takes time, energy, bandwidth and brain space.

We're turning on a torrent

The firehose of complexity and the downloading of data are coming at a great rate. Not just a firehose, a veritable torrent. Flowing rapidly, hard to stop or sip from.

Big data is growing

Big data is cool, it's hip and happening and now. But only those working with it really know what to do with it. The rest of us are looking at it from a distance trying to work out WTF to do with it. How can it help us? What do we look at? Which bits are relevant? How do we digest just a slice of it? How is it all connected?

Time is a wasting

Meanwhile, the clock's ticking, time is passing, clients and customers are waiting and competitors are snapping at your heels or worse, passing us. Productivity is needed; swift actions and resolutions are required to respond to VUCA, to remain agile, responsive, adaptive and competitive.

That presentation pack is a yawn

The information you're packaging up for your team, stakeholders, customers and colleagues is possibly a yaaaawwwwwwnnnnn! A PowerPoint slide deck full of bullet points, chevrons, arrows, boxes and clichéd phrases that make non-sense, no sense. It's not making sense. How do you expect people to make sense of a bunch of dot points?

Long meetings are losing focus

Teams in meetings are spinning in circles, trying to get out of an infinity loop of blah-blah. Wait a moment and you'll see people who have made some sense being drawn back in to the infinity loop by those who are yet to catch up or make sense of the data, the VUCA, the pack, the arrows, the torrent.

Stop the round and round

It's time for meetings, conversations, consultations and collaborations to stop being counter-productive, to stop the merry-go-round and round where it's hard to find where the exit is. The Ikea exit effect! How do I get out of this place? Where do we get off? How do we stop this thing? What do we do now? The sense maker, a sense maker, any sense maker steps in and helps bring clarity so there can be greater progress made and important work done.

Too long, dull and off target

The meeting model is flawed. And it probably wasn't even a model in the first place! That hour or two or three of your life that you'll 'never get back'. You know it when you walk from a talkfest where nothing was done but ego stroking, back slapping and knot untying. We humans were causing the complexity and ambiguity. Us. If we weren't causing it, we certainly weren't trying to untie the knot and make sense. So yes, we did contribute to it.

Our meetings are flawed.
There are too many of them.
They're too long.
They're dull and disengaging.
They start and move off target and head off on a tangent, never to return.
They're slow. Painfully slow.
Or they're steamroller slow - they make big heavy decisions and you don't know what's hit you.
Or they spin in circles out of control with the same content and phrases and beliefs being recirculated like stinky air in your car when you're following a truck spewing black smoke.

The 'they' of meetings is us. Meetings are of people.
We've got to fix the broken meeting model. And making sense can help.

More more more

Michael J Gelb in *How to Think Like Leonardo da Vinci* says the "information glut contributes to pervasive cynicism, fragmentation, and a sense of helplessness. We have more possibilities, more freedom, and more options than any people who have ever lived. Yet there is more junk, more mediocrity, more garbage to sort through than ever too." More more more. And it's *not* all good.

Blinders on

The ability to see possibilities is a powerful one, to see what might be possible, even though it's not visible right now. Or to come up with options, choices, ideas and innovations that can solve problems and propose work-arounds and solutions - that's genius!

Too many of us start the working day with our blinders on because we're not looking for possibility. We're wired for safety and sameness so to look out for something that might upset our apple cart isn't high on our 'like' list. If so many of us are wearing blinders, what's that doing for how well we're able to think about things? How does it impact how we think, communicate and create? How do our blinders restrict us from making sense? And how do they - worryingly - cause and create so much of the non-sense and ambiguity that we are struggling to make sense of today?

Now now now

Is it the goldfish effect: the idea that we have only a few seconds of attention span before we're looking for something else? Heck, we don't even want to wait for a webpage to load, or spend a few minutes to read through a LinkedIn profile - or worse a job application! We want things now, now and now. And we don't want to wait. A young woman was killed in my city recently because she didn't wait for the pedestrian lights to change. She dashed across on the 'red man', tripped, and a garbage truck coming around the corner (rightly, just following the traffic lights) ran her over. The shock of this tragic accident was felt throughout the city for weeks, months. She was in a hurry and life didn't wait.

Differences collide

Among the glut of information are different ideas from different minds and thoughts, colliding, trying to connect. What's it about? How does it relate to what we've already done? What should we do next? How does this bit connect to that? What do we do with it now? What do you mean? What are you saying? What do we keep? What do we throw out? What do we save until later? People are trying to work together in challenging VUCA circumstances.

Be more productive

With time ticking, the curse of the rework and the redo is debilitating. Wasted time, extra meetings and longer conversations trying to find the kernel of what this is about. We'd have moved on by now if we'd made sense of it quicker; we could have identified actions, started designing and crafting our responses, prototyping possibilities and testing some early versions with customers and users. It's not about being 'busy' it's about making good use of the time we have. Don't dick about wasting time talking about how it might be time or possibly a good opportunity to try and maybe, perhaps, possibly make sense …one day. Engage in deliberate sense making. Now!

Respect the quiet…

In our meetings, teams and conversations, there are often people who are quiet and don't contribute. They might hold back, they might be thinking a lot, but it's not coming out of them. Introversion and the power of the thinker in your team are well regarded. We need thinkers who think before they speak. But we also need to take the time to engage the quiet, to encourage collaboration and to listen extra carefully... for when the quiet DO contribute, they can be deafening with the sense, clarity and information they present. We can't be so quick to butt in on the quiet.

Making Sense is a life skill

Our ability to make sense of things must be a survival tool. We need it to make sense of toys, parents, school, learning, friendships, skills, sports, relationships, love, music, theatre, culture, difference, development, success ... in the right now as well as for the future.

Every day we're trying to make sense of stuff. Every little thing. Some of it we 'blow off' and let go, not bothering to make sense of, but other things we zoom in on and are determined to make sense of it so we can move on and proceed with some sanity and comfort ...among the anxiety producing VUCA.

It is an education or school thing?

Is making sense taught at school and throughout the education system? Is it part of learning, comprehension, mathematics, grammar, clear thinking or spelling? Do we learn to think about how we think? Do we learn to make sense in uncertainty and complexity?

Teachers could model it more

Ideally it would be in classrooms, and the teacher would model sense making. The learning would help students move from uncertainty to clarity. It would be so embedded in our learning that we would know how to 'do' sense making outside of school; in our family, our community, in sports, in social networks, in further study and in our first jobs and employment and right throughout our career. It would just be how we did things.

... and a part of every MBA

When MBA students are learning about economics and forecasting and modeling and innovation and trends, there would ideally be some sensemaking sitting alongside their studies. Just a part of how we do things around here. Integrated into every study, topic, piece of work and thinking. A sense making process so that learning is richer and outputs are shareable. Sense is made, sense is shared and those leaders take that knowledge and sense and continue to embed the practice in the workplace, in their community... wherever they are.

A business basic

Every member of the team needs to have the capability to play a sensemaking role; to step in at a moment's notice, to lead a conversation, to step up and just 'do' this as a part of the everyday. It's not a stand-out ... because it's the standard. We all have it, we all do it, the whole business and organisation and industry and community works this way. We are all sense makers and can step up to lead a sensemaking situation when it is needed.

A leadership imperative

If sense making and making sense is a business basic and there's more of it happening in schools and education, then we need leaders to really step on up and be leaders who make sense, and demand that sense be made. Sense making leaders wouldn't let gobbledygook survive. They'd call out clichés and put a stop to the waffle that ties sense making in knots. Leaders would require higher standards and they'd lead by example.

We are doing this non-sense

We've got to admit some harsh truths; it's us making the non-sense, and we can just as easily turn it to sense. Every time. We interrupt each other because we're not listening. We talk over each other because we're not listening. We sit in silence because we don't know what to do. We create misunderstandings because we're not listening or don't take the time to play back and reflect what someone says. We speak in different levels of abstraction. Some of us talk in big picture; some are deep down in the details.

Deeper learning

In workshops, meetings and conversations with sensemaking we'd be learning more. We'd be transferring knowledge, building our internal expertise and using Google for what is Google-able and each other for what's not. We'd experience deeper, richer learning, greater awareness and an awakening of sorts. Deeper listening. More knowing. More meaning. Making of sense. Doing of action.

Greater recall

Our short memories and two-second goldfish attention spans would lengthen. We would be calmer. We'd remember more and therefore be able to consider more. We'd give our brains more to do and we'd occupy them beyond tiring hormone firing and meaningless tasks.

Oh-so interesting and engaging

We'd be more interesting and engaging. Engagement scores would rise; the people we work with would be more interested and more interesting. More would get done, greater progress would be made and that means we could take on more without feeling the pressure or load. This seems paradoxical given the amount of data we're dealing with now.

Making Sense - Lynne Cazaly

Life looks real

With more sensemaking, we'd have a real look at life. We'd be making immediate sense of things, putting things in perspective, responding and dealing and remaining agile. We'd be present, not distracted. We'd be focused not pulled in different directions. We'd truly be getting to this place of authenticity that leaders are said to require to truly lead.

Lead, link and listen

Leaders would be leading, linking information and knowledge. They'd be listening. Really listening. And hearing. And absorbing and processing and making sense and meaning of all they're hearing. And then would come the sharing with their people and their teams. Connecting things for people, spreading knowledge and awareness. Building their influence to do the work that needs to be done. That's what leadership is.

Identifying themes

Trends, themes and similarities would be identified. Differences would be noted and connections would be made. We'd just do this sense making without making a big deal about it.

Rapid transmission

Ideas and segments of valuable information would be transmitted easily, virally and swiftly. They'd be digested and dissolved and integrated into projects and tasks and processes. We would learn. We'd integrate our learnings. They would be assimilated and it wouldn't feel clunky. If you wonder who ever has time to listen - when sense is made, listening is easier. Transmission is smoother.

Look, imagine

We would finesse our skills. It would happen in a Malcolm Gladwell *Blink* and it would be 'just how it happens around here.' We would see without thinking, we would think without talking, we would do without fighting. And we could reflect without thinking it needs to be a hippie activity. We'd reflect because we know that's what works. That's what helps dissolve and digest the meaning and helps make the sense.

Shaping the not yet knowns
The uncertainty would start to take form and shape. We'd feel less anxious and unsure. We'd be able to handle the VUCA because we'd have a way to process it, approach it and deal with it...swiftly. We'd categorise and sort and park and progress. We'd bring things to form that didn't previously have a form.

Engaging all types
We'd be connecting across cultures, languages and linguistics. We'd be drawing attention, focusing thinking and sharing meaning. No matter the location, the level of literacy or the experience in life, people would come together through knowledge, meaning and understanding. They'd be making sense… collectively. Collective sense making.

There would be human convergence
People would work, talk, communicate, engage, problem solve and live together... better. Instead of technology converging, humans would. Our thinking - although different - would be shareable, understandable, responsive and adaptive. It would transfer among us; it would build understanding and empathy. It would make our time here more palatable, productive, and purposeful. Perfect!

Diverse
Remote teams and people spread over multiple locations, different cities, towns, villages and offices. How do we get them on the 'same page'? What is the 'same page' anyway? Which

page is that? Different cultures, levels of literacy and language and local differences in tone, words, meaning and content. It can be more of factor in business than we might be realising. It might be slowing progress or causing non-sense because we're not dealing with it in a clear, concise and communicative way. Teams need to get together quickly and start working together, performing and delivering quickly.

Confusion - What is the problem anyway?

Among the complexity and ambiguity, we can be unsure of what problem we're actually solving. I saw a team last week head off on a tangent trying to fix something they knew they could fix, but it wasn't what the project or team needed. Yet they were so keen and desperate to do something. Anything. But it wasn't the right thing.

We create more nonsense in trying to work things out or in sharing our thinking while we're trying to work things out.

In writing this book, these were some of the discussions, rants and topics that cropped up in conversation with colleagues, clients and customers. What do you think...?

"Each and every day we need to influence and persuade others to our way of thinking or way of seeing the world, the problem, and the solution. At the end of these days, we need to sell our thinking, sell our ideas and sell our message so that others will buy it and buy in to it and ... do it."

Switching on to changes and trends

Making sense is a capability, an action and a behaviour that smart individuals, teams and organisation use for three main reasons:

- To remain competitive in a market
- To provide clarity of thought
- To guide a course of action

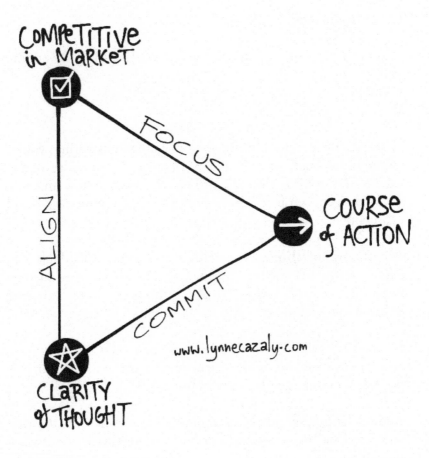

To remain **competitive in a market**, businesses and organisations need to keep a watch on trends, predictions and shifts along the broader landscape.

At a minimum, the model 'PESTLE' is a good one to give you some focus for what to be scanning and monitoring. You give some boundaries to what you're scanning across the areas of:
P - political factors
E - economic
S - social
T - technological
L - legal
E - environmental

… and you can go further to spell out 'STEEPLED' by adding in the factors of:
E - ethics
D - demographics

Whatever the acronym or the factors you're considering, you're scanning information and making sense of it so you're ready, willing and able to respond. When you make sense and you respond because of it, you're able to remain more agile and competitive.

For **clarity of thought**, making sense helps individuals and teams 'get across' lots of information and work out what they think about it. When you're scanning and gathering information, you're adding to the possibilities for future action.

If you've ever made a decision when you were feeling conflicted, confused or overwhelmed with information, it's possible you didn't make sense of things first.

And further, many people in organisations can hesitate to make a decision, or to even make a declarative statement about what they think.

Making sense is a pre-cursor to working out what you know and think and understand. Then you can share that with others. It's an entrée to decision making.

For a **course of action**, making sense provides great direction, insight and an increased confidence in times of uncertainty. It may not provide 100% certainty, but making sense can deliver enough certainty with which to act.

With fast changing business environments you often don't have the time, resources or luxury to wait until you know everything. And you can't. Because as soon as you think you know everything, the landscape changes; another factor from PESTLE or STEEPLED shifts and changes and you have new information feeding in to the situation.

Making sense gives a team, project and organisation enough clarity, competitiveness and knowledge about their next steps for a course of action. This is what makes it the perfect capability to get forward movement and momentum.

If you ever feel 'analysis paralysis' coming on, it's time to make sense of what you've got and plot your next steps and course of action.

And if you ever don't know what the *$%&# is going on, it's also time to make sense of what you have and work out where the gaps are.

If you're feeling like the underdog or like you have less of a competitive stronghold on a situation, it's time to makes sense to work out your next actions in response to what's happening.

Looking at the triangular model on the previous pages, you'll see that between *competitive in the market* and *clarity of thought* is **align**. When you're making sense, you're able to get things lined up, people in alignment, projects in parallel and resources harnessed and heading in the same direction.

Then between *competitive in the market* and *course of action* is **focus**. You can narrow your horizon, zoom in on your top five or top ten projects, strategies or pieces of work and pick up speed to head towards them.

And between *clarity of thought* and *course of action* is **commit**. When people know what's going on and know where they have to go, commitment is so much smoother, easier.

Troubles arise when we don't know what's going on, don't know where we're heading or don't know why we're working on something.

Help your teams, leaders and executives know what's going on; get aligned, focused and committed to a course of action. You'll be more competitive and the clarity of thought that comes from making sense will be sweet indeed!

"Many people spend time in activities like puzzles that call for insights because the act of struggling and then gaining understanding is so satisfying."

From 'Seeing What Others Don't: The remarkable ways we gain Insights'

- Gary Klein

Make Sense of What?

We need to make sense for ourselves as well as others.
Here's what we need to make sense of - for it, them and you.

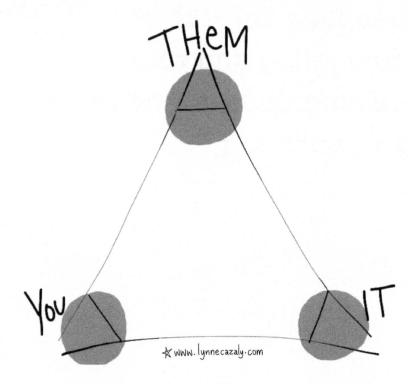

Make Sense of ... IT
The Wider World
In the market, industry, sector or field

- Competitor's actions
- Global shifts and changes
- Industry challenges
- Customer needs
- Social and community changes
- Technological changes
- Legislative impacts
- Policy changes
- Cloud something, anything.... everything!

Make Sense of... THEM
The Outer World
In a team, an organisation, at work

- The leadership message
- The organisational strategy
- Competitive position
- The changes to the strategy you're planning
- Organisational vision
- How the business is structured
- What that new leader is going to do and why they've been appointed
- The restructure you're about to announce
- The redundancies and retrenchments you're making
- The price rise in your products
- New customer needs
- Why the CEO resigned
- Changes in culture
- Customer feedback or complaints
- The reduction, change, alteration or shift in overtime, benefits or employee perceived perks

- Those new values
- Why you can only talk about some of the changes
- The buy out, merger, acquisition or ownership change
- The price rises
- Those changes to the organisation chart
- That legal case that no one is supposed to know about
- Those new printers or other technology
- Why that person was badly injured or killed in a safety accident
- Why no one is buying what you're making
- Why that product isn't selling as well as it used to
- Why your team isn't engaged
- The problems your stakeholders are having with <insert challenge>

✮ www.lynnecazaly.com

Make Sense of... YOU
The Inner World
For you

We're always working at making sense of our own situation, life, meaning of it and what to do next. How much are we battling the demons of yesterday? Just look at the power of *The Power of Now* by Eckhart Tolle and the self-development and reflection titles aimed at helping people get to grips with themselves and what to expect (or not) of themselves.

Making sense comes to the fore for us as individuals. You might say, think, or wonder:

* Is life panning out as I wanted?
* Why is this happening?
* What do I do about that?
* What does that mean?
* Oh shit! Now what?
* How do I get more of that?
* Is there a pattern here?
* Hang on a minute, this has happened to me before!
* Why does he/she keep doing that?
* Gee that annoys me when....
* Oh no, now what will I do? I wasn't expecting that! Faaaarrrrrk!

✷ www.lynnecazaly.com

"Blank stares often arise when someone has lost confidence that they can grasp—or should even care about—the idea you are communicating."

From The Art of Explanation: Making your Ideas, Products, and Services Easier to Understand

- Lee LeFever

Making Sense with Each Other

... Beware Epics, Train Wrecks and Bleeding Ears

The way we've been working isn't working.

To bring sense making to life any day of the week in any business, unit or organisation, I think it looks and sounds like this:

Imagine you're in a meeting, any type of meeting. We do so much of our work in meetings, or we TRY and do our work in meetings – talking with each other, problem solving, coming up with solutions, mapping things out.

When we're trying to work together and make sense of things, it doesn't always work out as we might like. Then the meeting gets the bad rap: you know, that meetings are useless, time wasting or purposeless. But it's the people IN the meeting who have made it that way.

So, whenever anyone contributes something in a meeting, there are a couple of ways to look at (and listen to) it to make sense.

There is the **content** that's being spoken of or discussed.
Add to that there is the **delivery** or the way that content is being delivered. And by being delivered, I mean speaking. People are talking. That's mainly what's happening in a meeting.

So it's the talking: *what* is being said... and *how* it's being said.

Let's take the **content**. It can be **clear**. That means when you hear it, it is distilled, it's filtered and it's fairly 'clean'.

Imagine water filters and the taste of water that comes through a water filter versus straight from a tap or a polluted stream or river. It tastes great. But at the other end is dirty water; it's content that is **tangled** and unformed. Almost no form; I'd call that amorphous. It has no shape or form. It could be non-sense or sense un-making as Brenda Dervin, sensemaking scholar and communication professor says.

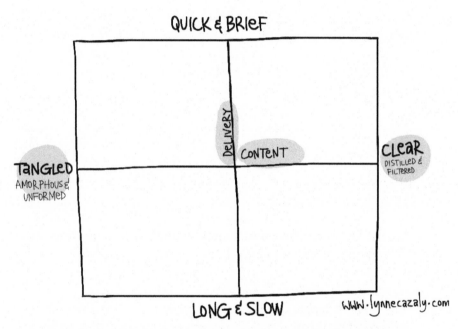

Crossing the content vertically let's look at the **delivery**, and how that information is being spoken about, delivered and presented.

There are people who deliver information and thinking and they are **quick and brief**. God bless them, they say what's needed and we can get on with things!

Making Sense - Lynne Cazaly

Then in contrast, there are **long and slow** delivery people. It takes a long time for the information and sense to be delivered. There's nothing wrong with that... it just is.

If you then check out each of the quadrants, you'll see (and hear) it all approaching... firstly the **train wreck**.

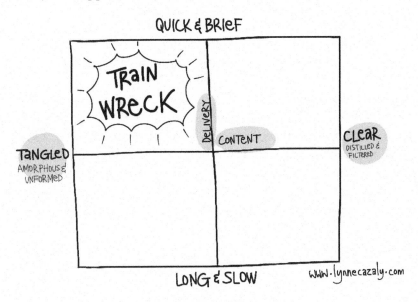

It's when you have someone speaking their train of thought. And that's good if that's what's been framed, arranged and is kind of 'allowed' in this situation. You just let people talk. This is not to say people can't speak their mind whenever they like. Often in workplace meetings we need to get our thinking focused, tight and articulated... and quick. You *can* just talk, but it's not a sense maker at work. It's tangled and that crash happens quickly. Once it's crashed, it's a tough recovery. You need a clean up operation before you can make more sense or good progress!

You can certainly allow the train wreck train of thought. Let it go and go and go.

Often we don't know what we think. Often the first version is not the final version. Speaking our mind is just that. This is a great 'first pass' - to let anything be said: to make it safe for anything to be landed on the table. It could be dangerous; it could be the opening and the start of something that is awesome. But you won't know unless you let it.

The skill here is to let... to allow, to let it go. Let. Yield. Give. Allow. But understand, it's possibly gonna be a train wreck.

Similarly when you have that tangled thinking and content being delivered in an unformed way and it's taking a L-O-N-G time, 'ouch I have bleeding ears. Your poor ears have to listen to all manner of crap. That ain't sense. That is non-sense. It can be so timewasting and counter productive. (Of course unless you have set up a 'get it off your chest session' where you just go for it and take as long as you like!)

But again, you can let it. You can let someone just go on. Let your ears bleed so bad that the person is heard; the full content of their thinking is captured.

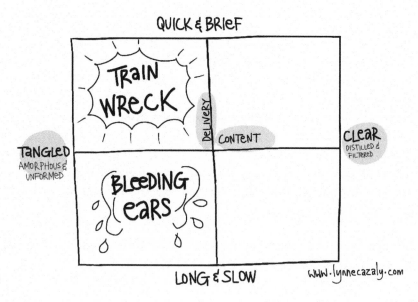

Making Sense - Lynne Cazaly

A colleague, Jacqui, who works as an interpreter listening to a presentation or conversation in one language and then relaying her translation in another language, often speaks of her 'bleeding ears'.

There are some languages, accents and tones of voice that are harder work than others. She has to focus and her ears are working over time, listening and sorting and classifying information, remembering and processing and translating. In amongst that she is dealing with the accents, intonations and unique features of that language.

"Oooowwwww my bleedin' ears," she'll say, at the end of an international conference, forum or meeting... and she's not swearing either!

Flip to the other side of this model; let's get some of that clear and distilled water. It may be clear but you can still have a l-o-n-g delivery time and duration. I reckon that's an **epic**.

There isn't a lot of time for epic masterpieces in the modern workplace. I think you need to schedule this time, to make it time boxed and targeted for this specific type of thinking and talking.

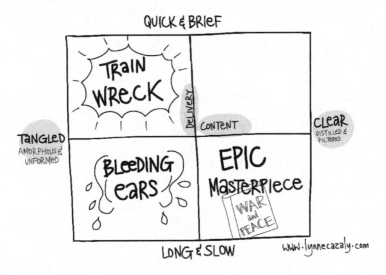

Make it clear that you're doing epic work by allowing the War and Peace type of presentation, thinking, discussing or non-sense making. It'll take time – be prepared for that.

The magic place to head for is **making sense**.

That means the delivery is quick and brief; the content is clear and distilled. You've got great message clarity. You've got swift delivery.

People receive the content quickly and then you can problem solve, discuss further or debate or decide or re-engineer or design or map out or whatever the next actions are.

Trouble happens when people are stuck on a train wreck or they're giving you bleeding ears. War and Peace just needs paraphrasing and editing.

Get to sense making as soon as possible so you can get on with the work of doing what you're making sense about. It looks like this:

Making Sense - Lynne Cazaly

A Path to Transformation

Using sensemaking techniques and approaches in work can lead to incredible transformation: in our people and what they do, for our customers and clients and right across the organisation and the communities you're connected to.

When you think of how confusing and complex things can get, making sense delivers a big return on investment.

So what does the path to transformation look like… or have the *potential* to look like?

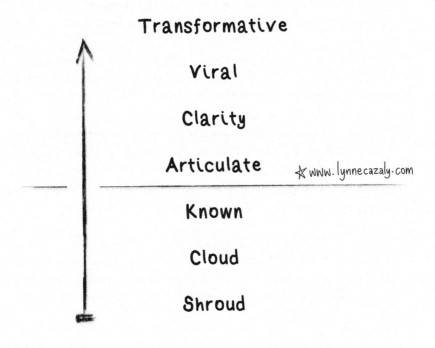

Transformative

Viral

Clarity

Articulate

☆ www.lynnecazaly.com

Known

Cloud

Shroud

Some organisations, teams or individuals can be in a **shroud**; hidden, covered or veiled from the facts, from reality. The approach of making sense isn't even on their radar. They're so smothered in details, embroiled in a crisis or in the process of winding up and closing their doors for good they're almost dead and buried!

It's just as a mountain gets covered in a shroud of mist where you can't see the top or peak; you may have seen the mountain during clear, sunny days and you know it's there, there is a summit, but exactly what it looks like, well... you're going from memory. Shrouding conceals things from view; obscures them.

Many leaders and teams do a busy job in business to shroud what they're doing and how they're doing it from the eyes of others. They're concealing information for survival. But sense making *is* a survival skill. We need to be doing better.

At times the shroud can lift, from a deep or heavy mist or fog, to clouds. It could be that information or people are in a **cloud**. The full picture isn't clear, perhaps a few pieces are.

The same happens with presentations of information in business; we only get part of the story - and it's the part filtered by the presenter. We're often given little if any chance to engage on the topic in a true two-way conversation or to influence or impact that filter.

Next in the path to transformation is **known**. It's a fairly standard place to be. There is a project, a piece of work, a priority or strategy and it's known. People talk about it, present about it, meet and waffle on about it and it's spotted, seen, observed and yep, it's that 'thing'.

When I asked a colleague in a financial services business what the project was she was working on she told me it was about making the financial adviser more efficient. She wasn't too sure what it did or how it worked, but she knew that one thing; it was about efficiency.

Now that's ok if you're only needing to transfer or share that type or level of information; but if she was working on the project with the team, I'd expect some further levels of knowledge.

We need to do better. And here is the tipping point; it's all a bit standard, a bit vanilla up to here. So let's go beyond and step into an area where organisational transformation is possible.

Stepping beyond just knowing is to be able to **articulate** that knowing. To be able to know it so clearly and succinctly that we can deliver information on that topic at a moment's notice. It truly is knowledge to us.

I like to watch how people respond when they've been asked to present something immediately or to respond to a question on the spot. It takes a while for the wheels in the mind to start whirring and deliver some sense to speak about! To be able to articulate information clearly and swiftly *is* sense making.

To build on the articulation and move towards **clarity** is sense making at work. To take a long story and deliver an executive summary, that's clarity.

It's about being able to distill to an essence and get clarity on a situation or a problem, a solution or a reason. It's a pleasure to listen and work with people like this.

And yet we can go further, to the point where that information is shareable. In whatever form, it becomes *viral*. People want to share it. It's easier to share it than keep quiet on it. Sense has been made... let's make sure more people know about it.

The true nature of a virus kicks in and Seth Godin's eBook *Unleashing the Idea Virus*, the most downloaded e-book ever, is an example. How viral was Seth's work? A book on how to spread ideas that was shared and spread across the world in rapid time, that's how viral it was!

With making sense, information and understanding is passed on and shared and we get to group sense making … to collective sensemaking… to collective sense.

And when an idea is shareable, it has really does have a power of *transformation*. Its time has come. That message, information, idea and concept can really do something. It can change what people think, say and do; how they make decisions, how they behave, what they value.

Transformation isn't achieved in shrouding or clouding. It's dangerous and often regretted later when the skies clear. Rather, it's the information or setting when things are known, articulated …and clearly. That's when making sense comes to life.

In workplaces, work spaces and mind spaces, sense making is a must. Beyond just telling people your thoughts or ideas or rattling on about what the problem is, help them make sense of it.

Distill it, dissect it. Make it digestible.

Make it easy to absorb, easy to share and easy to understand - that's what will transform a situation, a culture, a problem, team or organisation.

That's how making sense can bring about transformation.

The Future of Work

The world keeps changing.

In the words of the funk band *The Brand New Heavies* 'the world, the world, the world keeps on spinning yeah'. It does spin. And with it we do. Things keep changing. We keep changing. All of us, the whole thing continues to change.

So with this change is the technology that continues to be a part of every piece of our lives. The Internet of Things is more like the technology in everything.

We can ask Siri on our iPhone. We can check 'Help' on that website, we can ring a number for assistance; we can live chat now with a support person. We can ring someone to help us if we're feeling depressed and suicidal. We can check how much energy our air conditioner is using, we can track the performance of our vehicle, we can see how many steps and calories are on our wearable device today. We can Google my symptoms, a recipe, a TLA (three letter acronym) to wonder WTF it means.

As a child at school in the 1980s in was a little different: I remember would submit my enquiry and question to the librarian on a small index card. She would research it for me and the next week she would have some references for me to look at and read. I would write letters to companies asking for information on topics to include in my projects; two weeks later I received big envelopes via mail packed with juicy information and brochures.

My father sold the World Book Encyclopedia for a couple of years to create a supplementary income, so we had a set at our house. My studies and schooling seemed to lift up a notch with that in the house!

So if all this knowledge that was in a teacher's head or librarian's fingertips, is now Google-able, why am I needed at work, except for some labour? Diana Laufenberg's TED Talk *How to Learn: From Mistakes* unpacks this change in education nicely. Why indeed are teachers needed if the information has been given? Their role is transforming that's for sure.

In the future, cars won't need drivers, production lines won't need workers, kitchens won't need cooks and hospitals won't need doctors. Really? We're already taking photos of our ailments and sending them via apps to expert practitioners for advice and diagnosis. How much further is this going to go?

What will we need to know or do?

According to a report from *The Institute for the Future* titled *Future Work Skills 2020*, the top ten skills for the year 2020 are:

1. **Sense making**
2. **Novel thinking**
3. **Social intelligence**
4. **Trans disciplinary**
5. **New media literacy**
6. **Computational thinking**
7. **Cognitive load coping**
8. **Cross cultural competency**
9. **Design mindset**
10. **Virtual collaboration**

Published in 2011, the report provides a neat summary of each. For sensemaking it reads:

"Sensemaking: the ability to determine the deeper meaning or significance of what is being expressed".

Linked to sensemaking is **novel thinking** and **cognitive load coping**. In fact all of these skills are linked to the number one skill of making sense out of 'WTF is going on' and 'what are we gonna do about it'! It's the 'what do we think', and 'what they said, what we're wondering, what those hunches are and how it could all work together'.

That's making sense.

A summary of the report was also presented in an article in Forbes magazine with a quote from Steve Jobs reading: *"Creativity is just connecting things. When you ask creative people how they did something, they feel a little guilty because they didn't really do it, they just saw something"*.

Think about dot connecting. The phrase 'connect the dots' is part of the language we might use; we're looking to find a way of making sense from a bunch of data and information. Connecting the dots of data, the dots of results and information is what we need, crave, want and strive for.

Bernard Salt from KPMG at a Future of Work conference and from a report on Australia's Nationwide Broadband Network (GenNBN) said the future of work would be fluid. And those being born now will know only a digital world.

Salt believes we will be flexible and fluid in our working; we will work in an office two days a week and then we'll be in our tree change or sea change location the other three days of the week.

More than ever we will need to get to grips with information and make sense, quicker than ever before.

Salt suggests you'll do work at different hours, a few here and there. It will be more flexible; you'll have control over when and where you work. And the types of jobs we have will be different.

Over recent years there's been an increase in health and allied services jobs, education and knowledge worker jobs.

How do we future proof ourselves for the future of work?
The skills we will need are softer. We'll need skills of fluidity, flexibility, and sociability.

The fluid workplace will be the workplace of the future and rather than holding a rigid view of your skill set you'll need to 'fit in' to a new role, job, position and workplace.

We'll all need to be more agile, fluid, flexible, responsive, adaptive, spontaneous, willing, yielding, changing – this is what will future proof our careers and lives for the future. Nothing is stable.

We need to be able to survive and thrive in this fast moving interconnected and VUCA world. Yet we sill need to have the skills that will enable us to deliver, to prosper and contribute in a way that's meaningful for us and purposeful for the those we serve and help.

In a way it means we'll have more control over us, ourselves. For the control freaks among us, that's satisfying because all the talk of that uncertainty stuff is freaking plenty of us out!

Leaders Need to Evolve Too

The days of the leader being directive 24/7 are gone; leadership has shifted to being more **consultative**. And it will evolve further to leaders being **facilitative**, being able to draw information, ideas and insights out of the team rather than telling, instructing or adding.

I see the telling role has shifted from just sharing information where the onus is on the giver of information to the role of **eliciting** information. Here the onus is on the leader or facilitator. They draw information out through communication, questioning and eliciting techniques. That's what builds engagement.

We're shifting from an information economy, to a knowledge economy, to the next world where it is all about the **meaning** you make and create.

History has shifted: data is the thing of the decade. It's next going to evolve to making **sense**. How do we make sense of data? It's how we make sense of the past as well as the present.

From teamwork to collaboration and now shifting and evolving further to teams **co-creating** and working with customers, clients, colleagues and others from diverse fields.

We're evolving from collating and creating ... we're now the **curators** of our own galleries of information, our own Instagram and Facebook photo albums. And from play, to gaming, it's now about **improvising**; we're in uncertainty remember, the rules of any said game may not apply.

THEN 1.0	NOW 2.0	NEXT 3.0
Directive	Consultative	Facilitative
Tell	Share	Elicit
Information	Knowledge	Meaning
History	Data	Sense
Teamwork	Collaboration	Co-creation
Collate	Create	Curate
Play	Game	Improvise

✱ www.lynnecazaly.com

The role of leaders is changing; leaders need to evolve.

Making Sense - Lynne Cazaly

The Leader as Collaborator and Facilitator

Meeting with a client yesterday and we were talking about how leadership continues to change and evolve. So the 'leadership is evolving' conversation went like this:

Leadership used to be **directive**: 'you... do this'.

It's evolved to being **consultative**: 'would you like to do this?'

And continues to evolve to more **facilitative**: 'what's your view on what needs to be done? How will we go about doing it?'

Of course the questions will differ depending on the team, situation and needs of the business, but the shift and change is clear. From strong, directive statements, to questions about the work to be done, to a more facilitative, eliciting style of leadership.

I think we may fear the facilitation style of leadership, thinking that it's going to take too long. *"Who's got time to ask all those questions!?"* Even the consultative style of leadership can be perceived as being a lengthy approach to achieving an outcome. *"It's just quicker for me to tell them what to do."*

Yeah? How much do you like being told what to do? Our **tell** bank accounts have a small balance in them. I think you need to save your directive approaches and telling for when they're really needed.

We need to use consultative approaches more, and realise they won't take longer... in the long run. If you're getting impatient or it feels like you're not getting anywhere, you'll likely save time later by getting buy-in, connection and engagement now, and to leverage that right throughout the process of leading the team.

Plus, facilitative styles of leadership put more responsibility on the individuals and the team.

The leader has less of the answers, which means less telling, less direction. This helps boost collaboration, trust, engagement, interest and freedom.

Yes you'll still need to 'lead', to manage performance and to handle the tricky stuff when it comes up, but leadership continues to evolve and so must we, if we are to engage and inspire coming generations and diverse cultures.

And so with this change in leadership, the change in the way of working, the volatility, uncertainty, complexity and ambiguity, it's on the leader to kick off the sensemaking... to allow, enable and facilitate the making of sense – whenever and wherever it's needed. What do you think?

Knowledge Workers as Sense Makers

Mr Drucker said it last century; it's all about the knowledge. It was 1969 when Peter Drucker sliced knowledge workers away from manual workers and foretold that it would be knowledge workers getting most of the work. The information based economy and all that.

But many of us still do a bit of both; some knowledge work and some hard manual labour. Robotics and technology have picked up some slack, but it's as if we need our brains, insights, knowledge and human understanding more than ever.

The sharing of information across organisations is increasing - and it should. Transparency will help in understanding, collaboration, creativity and innovation. The rise of visual management to plan, measure, implement and review is a powerful part of leadership and management.

When team and organizational data is put on show, everyone can tap into it. You can see how you contribute, how you're interconnected and how what you do impacts others.

Among a list of icebreaker games used to warm up a group, room or team, is a sweet one using a ball of wool or string. (And a footnote of sorts, I can't stand those party game types of icebreakers that are about breaking balloons and passing oranges. Cringe!)

This one involves the group standing in a circle and the first person leads off, holding onto the end of a ball of string or wool. They might say something, an insight or expectation or introduce themselves or some other wonderful gem... and then they throw the ball to someone else across the circle. Note they keep hold of some of the wool and throw the ball on... and on it goes, zig zagging across the circle. At the end, the string is crisscrossing that circle.

You can pull on the string from where you are and it will tighten for others; lift the string up or down, lifting your arm up and down and again, the pressure and connection is felt throughout the group.

It shows that even when you do something that you think might be individual, just affecting you...in fact no, we're all connected. The impacts of our work, efforts and actions are felt across the circle, around the circle.

The same applies to us all, in our roles, in our teams, units, organisations, industries; we're all part of a greater system, and we too often forget that.

Know that whatever you do, with whatever information or knowledge you get, have or share, you can and will be having an impact on others.

So what is this 'Knowledge Work?'

For many people, understanding knowledge work takes a little knowledge. In short it's about communication and collaboration.

Peter Drucker predicted that industrial and mechanical approaches to work and doing hand crafted, man-made work would taper off. He suggested that knowledge work and knowledge workers would be a big part of the future. (Mind you, I think we're experiencing the resurgence of the value of hand crafted, artisan and man-made work; the individuality of it, the 'tailored just for you' of it. But back to knowledge work for a moment...)

Knowledge workers are voracious learners, open to new information and to processing that information. They are innovative and focus on the quality of work produced, not just the numbers or quantity. This is because knowledge work often doesn't produce anything tangible that you can grab hold of; it's largely invisible.

Different to those in manufacturing for example - we make something, it's sitting there at the end of the conveyer belt and it drops into a cardboard box and is shipped off to a customer.

For many knowledge workers, there is little specificity. Work is broad based, holistic and looking at how things are changing across a broad spectrum. It's a question-based area of work; less about answers, more about thinking, wondering, asking questions, uncovering, connecting and linking.

Status Quo = Dirty Word

Let's have a look at those who love working with information and making sense.

Are you one of them? Do you know one? Want to be one? Do you work with one... or more?

You can know information in an organisation, but what happens to it? How is that information connected with other information and other people across the business? There are knowledge technologists who do awesome work with their hands. Think manufacturing, computing and technology.

Knowledge isn't skill. Skills can change slowly over time. Knowledge can be out of date overnight. So the idea that knowledge workers need to continuously learn is refreshing and reassuring. The other side of learning is teaching and so sharing that knowledge, information, meaning and sense is an important part of the knowledge worker's legacy.

Knowledge workers are independent, yet interdependent. They are somewhat of a DIY or do-it-yourself kind of person; they have to look after themselves, their development, learning, progress.

The more we can know about how we work, think, collaborate, innovate, process and create ... the better.

Organisations with knowledge workers need to let go of the leash. Times have changed; leadership is continuing to evolve. Control isn't cool. Control is a killer.

It's these knowledge workers who bring the creativity, innovation and possibility to a team and organisation. They forge new paths, find new ways, think new things and make new connections. Hooray for them! Hooray for you! They find problems to solve and churn out solutions that you didn't know you needed. They think, therefore they are.

Best of all, knowledge workers are sharers. Once they've cottoned on to a line of thinking or a train of thought, they're at the ready to share it and shape it and co-create it with others. Then it can take off and have a life of its own.

They want feedback, they want to test it out, try it on, see how it feels and wonder what could be beyond this.

So the status quo = dirty word.

In the words of Frances Horribe, knowledge workers are 'individuals who use their brains more than others do'. Cheeky? Perhaps. Rather, he means they're using their heads more than their hands.

Making Sense - Lynne Cazaly

So there you have knowledge workers; they're thinking away and they're doing lots of interpreting and wondering and they're asking questions. I think those questions can ruffle feathers around businesses. They may well be provocative, or play the devil's advocate with their questioning; they're not trying to unseat you or trying to trick you out, they seriously want to know more, understand why or what or how something works... or doesn't work.

They are private investigators of sorts. Hunting out information, finding connections, digging deeper and looking wider. They are curious. They are sense makers and facilitators of making sense.

If you hear someone say 'our people are our greatest asset' - you could insert the phrase and make a little edit there: 'our knowledge workin' people are our greatest asset.'

I don't think there are two knowledge workers alike. It's the path they've taken to get to here that makes them unique. And in the sphere of thinking for a living, their thinking as well as the path to getting here makes them truly individual. It's that type of diversity that *helps* an organisation, not hinders it. Diversity isn't just about culture or race or age or sex. It's diverse thinking, wondering, views and perspectives too. That helps with the making of sense.

And there's high potential for a bit of free and easy when you're hanging around or working with some knowledge working people. Every day may be different. Creativity and innovation abound. How totally refreshing!

You'll notice or know a knowledge worker because they like:

- **Autonomy**. They'll often prefer the opportunity to work, think or be alone, musing over the possibilities of the information and knowledge.

- **Opportunity**... to approach work in a free flowing or open style. Who knows what might happen or what might be the best way to handle things... plus, it could all change and look a whole lot different once we get started!

- **Watching and observing**. So much can be gained by people watching, listening, looking, processing, observing, distilling and pattern finding; and

- **Knowledge**. They love what they're thinking about, wondering about and posturing over. It really is a labor of love.

Knowledge workers – either by title, role or interest – are critical players in the making of sense.

If you are one, congratulations; you have important work to continue doing.

If you know one, understand them and their approaches to working with knowledge, and people.

And if you're yet to be one... hang on. You're likely to be evolving into one for the future of work.

Getting on the same page

How often do people say 'let's get on the same page' or 'are we on the same page'?

So which page exactly is that?

Getting people to understand or see what something is really about can be a challenging conversation or meeting and it can take a period of time. Sometimes it can take you a long time.

What's that idiom or saying about information is power and the person who has the information is the all-powerful one?

In earlier days of work, pre technology and Google Docs and S drives, the holder of the information was the records manager. Compactus files of manila folders and spring bound stationery junkie folders held reams of printed pages.

Employee records manager - ooooh, great holder of power.

Finance manager - lots of power, so many invoices, lots of remittances and those individually printed cheques.

At least it sat in a central repository. You knew it was somewhere in the organisation; you could go and search through it, just like actors in television programs and series when they head off down to 'Records' to uncover crucial information so they can solve a cold case or crime. You knew where it was. It had physical form.

Information is curiously becoming more plentiful and at the same time less accessible. Yes it's residing in the cloud via a networked computer somewhere but it can be a little harder to actually see. It's easy to share when you know where it is, but if everyone can access it, why don't they?

With plenty of places to get the information, why are many people still feeling disconnected, ill-informed and out of the loop? I believe we all have a job to do as well as our job and that is to share, to connect, to collaborate and to make sense.

Even if we don't feel like it.

We all need to take responsibility to put information and sense in places where people can stumble upon it. It needs to be visible, to be radiated and distributed - not just as an attachment, not just as a link, but visible, seen and absorbed.

We need transparency

That word 'transparency' is used in governance, leadership, performance and planning.

But how transparent is your thinking and information?

How well can you see through what you're thinking so that you can communicate, share and spread that thinking?

It can take too long to get our heads around what others are thinking; it feels like thinking is opaque, cloudy and thick ... rather than transparent, clear and simple.

That's why getting on the same page is such a requirement yet such an effort at times.

Too often in an effort to get on the same page, we resort to lazy methods like lists and clumps of unsorted information, expecting others to do the sensemaking.

We can do better.

Bullet Points are Bullshit

Many a leader embarks on a piece of communication, a presentation or a sense making exercise by compiling a bunch of bullet points.

"These are the points I want to make; I'll put them on a list."
"And another list. And another."

Slide after slide this goes on. Yaaawwwwwn!

"Pull the plug! Go on I dare you! Step out from behind the PowerPoint slide deck you've created."

This is what I said this to a leader of a major change initiative in a health insurance business and he said ...'No. I can't do that!!!'

But if you're rolling out your communications and key messages for that change and transformation project you're working on - just as this leader was - you don't need a slide deck, a pack or a bunch of pages with boxes, arrows, chevrons and bullet points in it.

In fact those bullet points you've got there? They're bullshit.

There. It's in print.

I think bullet points are bullshit.

And here's my PowerPoint slide to prove it:

They don't help with making sense.

They boring, linear, impossible to memorise after about five - unless you're a memory champion - and they do little to inspire or inform, particularly during times of change.

Most of all, bullet points often show up as a default option in PowerPoint. But you need to buck the default if you want to get engagement and understanding with your message and help people make sense of detail, complexity and dense information.

With all of the information flying around your organisation and team, you want your change messages to get a little more cut-through than the notice in the kitchen that says "cleanliness is everyone's responsibility!"

Just because you have some key points to make about change, doesn't mean they need to be communicated as points.

Unpack your entire message across different dimensions.

You could tell a story or cite some data.

You could quote someone else in the business or industry or show the chart or map of the rollout plan.

You could explain where things were and what they'll be like in the future.

You could ask some engaging questions or present some customer insights. You could have a conversation with customers or clients.

How about sharing some information on the trends in the industry...

You get the 'point' don't you?

All of these elements help people connect the dots, make sense and get a clearer picture of what's going on. A list of bullet points is lazy. It's not a sensemaking tool.

So back to this leader I challenged to 'pull the plug'...

We took his PowerPoint pack of bullet points and crafted some flip charts, posters, key messages, a couple of stories and some questions so that he could have dialogue with the team.

And that's what he rolled out across the country - no PowerPoint in sight.

He did pull the plug; and his people were so pleased he did. He stepped out from behind the dense pack of white A4 pages or stark screens of projected text-heavy slides.

Now he's talking, engaging, interacting and co-creating the change process with his team. That's leadership and that's human sensemaking. That's collective sensemaking. He's brining people together and together they're making sense.

Hooray!

Keep fear out of the picture

Making sense has such a place in this VUCA world because it's freakin' scary out there. And in here come to think of it, inside our minds too!

But this is how we make our representation of the outside world… the images and pictures we create in our mind, our imagination, and our perception.

So it makes sense that we could use an image or picture of sorts: a map, a visual sense or a way of connecting some dots and understanding what's happening to help us make sense. It actually helps calm us down.

Deborah Ancona in her work on sensemaking says that a map gives us something to hold onto which in turn keeps fear at a distance.

You'll know from going on a road trip anywhere that it's helpful to know where you are, where you're going and 'when do we get there?' It helps reduce uncertainty, which is just a watered down version of first-grade fear.

Ancona tells the story of a troop of soldiers who were lost in the Swiss Alps. They didn't know where they were and then… it began snowing. Struggling to find out where they were, they were doing their best with problem solving to try and create a solution.

A little later one of them found a map in their pocket and with relief they were able to work their way through the map and find their way out of the snow, out of their lost state and into safety.

It turns out the map was of the Pyrenees, not the Alps!
They were lost in the Swiss Alps remember?

Making Sense - Lynne Cazaly

The map solution shows that, as sensemaking elder Karl Weick says, 'any old map will do'.

The soldiers had purpose, says Ancona and they had focus and they were heading somewhere.

The map was a start. And a start for focus relieves and reduces anxiety.

With sense making, once you're on your way, just pick up the cues; keep making sense and all will be good.

Any old map will do.

And as that sweet quote from the film *The Best Exotic Marigold Hotel* said: 'It'll be alright in the end, and if it's not alright, it's not the end'.

So it's true with making sense too.

Keep going.
There's more up ahead.
It will never be totally 'right', or 'all right'.

There will be more; it's not the end.

Just keep going. It will be ok. You'll get more information soon which will help you update your sense … and you need to get comfortable with that.

"Certain problems benefit from a linear and rational approach, while other, less straightforward challenges—navigating in a fog—benefit from the problem solving utilized in the human sciences like philosophy, history, the arts, and anthropology.

We call this problem-solving method sensemaking."

From 'The Moment of Clarity:
Using the Human Sciences
to Solve Your Toughest Business Problems'

- Christian Madsbjerg, Mikkel B. Rasmussen

Making Sense - Lynne Cazaly

how to make sense

"Once you move your attention in a certain direction you can easily see what is there to see but, the decision to move your attention could take twenty years!

... You have to direct your own attention."

From 'English Thinking: The Three Methods'
- Michael Hewitt-Gleeson

It's a system thing

Dr Edwards Deming knew what it was all about... it was all about systems.

Known as the System of Profound Knowledge (SoPK), Deming was at it his whole life.

A theory of management, this system put forward a framework of thinking and action for leaders of all levels – as long as they were committed to making change, transforming how things were and wanting to create a thriving, pulsing organisation that worked for everyone connected with it.

He took a whole systems view of things; not one or two things in isolation... all of it, together. All of the elements and pieces working together to achieve the end result.

He suggested we ask questions like:

- *Why did something go wrong?*
- *Why isn't this working as we thought?*
- *How can we repeat this?*

In Deming's view, opinion wasn't fact. He wanted us to test our theories, our ideas and opinions; to find the data and understand WTF is going on so we can improve on it.

For many people, Deming's PDSA model:

- *Plan*
- *Do*
- *Study*
- *Act*

is more mantra than framework; they're able to live their lean, systems, agile, development, progress or growth projects by that cycle; project after project, piece of work after piece of work.

For making sense, be prepared to look across the whole system, even if it seems unrelated or unconnected. It truly is a system thing.

★ www.lynnecazaly.com

Starting by speaking up

The word 'plausible' crops up in sensemaking - we need a plausible understanding of the world and how it's changing to make sense.

Plausible. It means reasonable or believable, probable.

For many people, it's about mapping things. And then you go ahead and test the map out with others. To put the map together you may have collected some data and information, you may have had conversations with people, and you may have read and distilled information. Then once you've got your map, you go again. More conversations, reading, thinking, distilling. And the map gets changed. The map may even get deleted!

The reason why sense making makes so much sense is that it helps us get to grips with the unknown.

When you think of VUCA (volatility, uncertainty, complexity and ambiguity), many of this is unknown. But you've got to do your best to make some sense of it. It's the basis of contemporary workplace practices like meetings and workshops and innovation and product development.

So Karl Weick says sense making helps us structure the unknown. He specifically says we can put stimuli into a framework. It's that which helps us understand the unknown. It isn't just thinking. It's a doing word or an action that's for sure. It's about words, talking, conversations, collaboration, reasoning, wondering, deducting.

Once you've done the sense making, it's about getting into action.

For many the challenging part of making sense is trying to put that abstract or unknown into words. You know when you can't explain something - maybe it's complex or complicated or it's so 'out there' or abstract or conceptual that it doesn't really have a meaning or a definition yet.

But it's not until you start trying to put some words around it that it will start to make sense. You'll hear yourself speaking, trying to make sense. Others will hear you, they'll start to make sense.

The unknown starts to take shape or get some form about it.

It's a gutsy thing. It's bold and courageous and in the title of Brene Brown's book (and Ted Roosevelt's quote) it is indeed 'daring greatly'. You might be a lone voice; you might be a devil's advocate and you might be drawing attention to an elephant in the room... or an elephant that's walking up the road a few kilometres away; they're not even in the room yet, but you're seeing something, you're wondering something.

We need leaders, workers, humans who are willing to speak out when they're making sense of things. Their actions will help others. It's a human need for us to know. To know why.
Think young toddler, asking 'why' repeatedly. They're trying to make sense of things. This continues our entire life. Connecting disparate pieces of information, trying to make links, understand, interpret.

Given the uncertainty and unknowns in the world of work, making sense of things is an ongoing, daily activity. There's so much to look at, learn and absorb.

In Deborah Ancona's work on sense making there is the explanation that you might go from simple to complex and back to simple again. I think when you're in the complex zone, people can feel disconnected or feel it's 'hopeless'. Some of the team or group may have a feeling of wanting to give up: 'it's all too hard' or 'we'll never work this out' or 'this is just bigger than we are.'

You hear huffs and puffs and whispers and... silence. You see blank faces, dejected expressions, eyes that are puzzled or glazing over.

But before long you might find that through sense making you're out of simple, into complex and out of complex heading over to simple again. Aaaaaah, clarity! That's what it feels like.

Stand by though... more complexity is around the corner. It's never really 'done'. The reason we move from complex to simple and back again is that while we're thinking and talking and working and wondering, new information, data and ideas are coming to light. People are doing stuff and the consequences are felt. So the situation changes. It's never 'done.'

So off we go again; more sense making. And some deeper levels of learning, understanding and more information we can make sense of and act on.

I think this is why it truly is one of the most critical skills in today's workplaces and will become even more critical as work continues to transform, change and evolve.

The Wonder of Weick

Karl E Weick is considered by many to be the grandfather or godfather or senior figure, thought leader and one of the leading thinkers and publishers on sense making.

His writing and research is certainly compelling. His book *Sensemaking in Organisations* is comprehensive for sure.

As I read anything of Weick's I find myself nodding, highlighting and notating, saying to myself 'yes, this is important'. Next thing you know, I have a whole page highlighted to focus on and revisit. His conclusions and insights just... make sense.

He has also contributed to numerous papers and journal articles. A full list of the references I've read and reviewed in putting this book together is listed at the end, but Weick, in his book, cites over 500 references. That's some reading Karl! And that's where you can go if you want even more, to explore further, to add to the making of sense on sense making.

Weick says that meanings materialise - not like magic, but through language, talk and communication.

It's like looking at the current state, seeing there is a gap, and then up ahead is the future or desired state. It's so often how business strategy is talked about, but not often enough is making sense a deliberate part of the strategy.

Small is not insignificant.
It could be a ripple of magnificent change.

A BIG question Weick says we need to be asking is:

What's the story?

He suggests we consider the small, subtle moments, as well as the conspicuous and the large. That's why listening to quieter voices is important. Little can have a big impact.

Weick says we could ask: 'What's the story here? Now what should I do?' This helps bring meaning into existence.

There can be 'clusters' of information or cues that get your attention. Perhaps you can't put your finger on it but there they are.

Weick says that sense making starts with chaos. That's a relief in a way. Because that's when we need it most, when things are a tad crazy. From the chaos you draw out or extract some cues.

So you start by noticing... noticing what's normal. What doesn't fit? From this you can begin to find a new meaning, invent a new meaning, via interpretation.

Weick speaks of 'bracketing'; we put something around it, based on our existing mental models. We give it some type of meaning or response. The bracket is like a net – you can somewhat relax, you've put something around all that information and made some meaning or sense from it, or out of it.

Sensemaking uses 'labeling'. Labeling finds common ground yet it kind of ignores the individual views people have of things. It's important your labels have some 'plasticity' as Weick says. Things have to be able to be moved, shifted, changed and adapted. That's just how sense is.

In a story in Weick's work about a nurse working in the care of a patient and monitoring their vitals, this brilliant quote comes forth: 'how can I know what I think until I see what I say'... and in medical ways, 'how can I know what I'm seeing until I see what it was?' Think of medical data produced by machines, the measuring, the beeps, the numbers and the charts.

Sensemaking follows action.

One of my favourite quotes from Weick's work, where he quotes Paget... "**Now** represents the more exact science of hindsight, **then** the unknown future coming into being."

In sense making we're trying to connect that indefinable abstract up there, to the deep details that are concrete and now.

Think of it like a ladder. How is the top rung connected to the bottom? By some rungs in the middle and the two planks or bars on the side - they are the sense making.

Sensemaking is happening across your organisation, community, industry, sector, government, country... it's happening where everyone is. What's terrifying for example, is that it's happening all over the organisation but it's not connected.

Disparate parts and silos busily making sense. Alone.
That's the big worry. We need to come together, right now folks. Now.

Above all sense making is about action. Those questions from Weick again:

What's going on here?
What do I do next?

Talking and action. When we're sense making we are constantly iterating, changing, building, developing, growing, shifting that understanding. It can't help but be shaped and shifted when we talk about it.

And Weick points out that action and talk aren't linear. You don't do one, and then the other and you're done. You keep doing them.

Making Sense - Lynne Cazaly

It's cyclical.

You go around and around … not in circles but with sense making.

Go around again.
More talk, more action.
Go again.

The Past

Hooray for Weick's comments that adaptive sense making means we will both honour and reject the past. Beautifully said! The past was there, we make sense of it and now we reject it for the now which will soon be the next past.

Surely you've been in a meeting where some people just couldn't get past the past? I don't blame them. We shouldn't expect them to. It's an important connection with the future.

Next time, honour it, honour the past, give it some due, but then reject and look at the next - which will soon be the past.

The C-word

The c-word in sense making is Communication. This is what is at the guts of sense making and making sense. That's what we're doing day in and day out. Engaging and communicating with people trying to work out what's going on and what to do next. It's about the talking, the listening, and the communication.

Another C-word is 'Capability'.
Sensemaking: it's a key leadership capability.

The MIT Sloan School of Management and their 4Cap model of leadership capabilities says it's about sense making, relating, visioning and inventing.

To me these sound like the Future of Work skills... these are the things that leaders need.

Think it, speak it, hear yourself saying it.

Then you'll know just how much you understand it.

Making Sense - Lynne Cazaly

An act of courage

Making sense is a courageous act, as Deborah Ancona explains in her paper on leadership capability. When you come to say or spit forth what you're making sense of, the talking part, you can bet that some courage is required to speak out.

Yes speaking out about what you're thinking or wondering or seeing takes courage. You may not have the popular view. You may not have the right answer either, but you owe it to yourself, the market, your organisation, your customers, users and stakeholders to speak up and out when you're making sense of something. You need to let people know what you're thinking and seeing.

Authors and speakers like Brené Brown and Margie Warrell are all about courage, vulnerability, bravery. Their personal commentaries from their own lives and research translate beautifully to the work world.

I think there's a little 'Beware' sign… it doesn't say 'Danger' or 'Keep out'… it's just 'Beware'. Be aware that proceeding with active and explicit making of sense is a courageous act. Good on you. Go for it. It's needed.

It's truly about having the courage to articulate what you're thinking, what you're hearing, what you're wondering. This is a social thing. You're bringing into the open what has been hiding in your head. Aaaarrrgggghhhh, this could be tricky! This could be risky. This could be dangerous. Will you survive? Your lizard brain wonders this before you even open your mouth. It chooses and perhaps offers wise counsel to either go ahead or press 'pause' on your thinking.

Your random (possibly unrelated) thoughts are now going to hit the airwaves so others can hear them. It's like you're switching on the microphone at a radio or television station and that big red 'ON AIR' light is gonna flash. Everyone... here it comes. Aaaah, rather, hear it comes!

You're about to deliver the information that is relevant, connected, simple, concise, rambling, uncertain, detailed, succinct, unrelated, whatever.... here it comes. Here with it comes courage.

At the end of the day, or at the start of the chaos - whichever comes first - sense making is born from disruptive ambiguity, so says Weick. You notice something. You bracket it. You look back, you look forward. You wonder. You presume. You act. With others.

You ask 'what's the story?' and you ask 'now what?'
And you watch what happens next....

There is so very much more of Weick's work that could be quoted, cited and commented on. It's not often you read a book or journal article and line after line you want to highlight everything, because it's ALL important or it's ALL relevant to what you're thinking of and working on, or you just love it all so much. That's how I feel reading and referring to Karl Weick's work. That's why I believe he has created a wonderful world... a truly wonderful world of sensemaking.

It was the worst of times...

Yes sad but true, we often need our best sense making capabilities when we can least deliver them: in times of a crisis or when the 'shit has hit the fan'.

When things are changing rapidly and we don't know what's happening we can go all rigid-like. That's not helpful. We've got to stay malleable, flexible, open, responsive and able to take in information.

In my earlier career in communications and public relations, sensemaking would particularly kick in when it was crisis time. I worked in a community relations role in a public hospital for several years, liaising with media, medical and nursing staff, supporters and volunteers, community stakeholders and ... the community, both internal and external. It was a rewarding role and it was curiously thrilling. Advances in medicine and treatments saw the first CT scanner come to the hospital after a mega fundraising appeal. Nuclear medicine was on the scene and progressive surgical advances were being made with short stay surgery and clinical and allied health.

Then there was that day... make it that week from hell ... when the bacteria, commonly known as Golden Staph broke out in - the midwifery or new mum's ward. Oh no! This isn't good. Where new babies are?! And new mums and dads and families?! What the?

Golden Staph and many other bacteria live in hospitals in manageable levels, mostly; that's the job of the Infection Control Unit team. But this time, it was rife, out of control, spreading and it was crisis time.

Speaking to the media when you don't have all the facts is absolute sensemaking. They're asking questions and the medical and support teams are still finding out things. You run a schedule of rolling media conferences so you can tell what you know as soon as you know it.

There were new mums and dads to take care of, new babies to protect, staff who needed to keep delivering services across the hospital and they needed protection too. It really was the worst of times.

Making sense in times of challenge is certainly a leadership capability. Deborah Ancona says that if we're able to make sense of things and calm down a bit, that can be better for us than searching endlessly for the 'right' answer. We can relax because the right and final answer will never be found. We have to do our best to find the *current* best answer.

Most of all it is a ***doing*** activity. It's not just a ***thinking*** or a ***talking*** thing. You've got to actually DO something to then see after a while if that was helpful or had an impact or if it didn't quite result in what you were hoping.

Ancona explains that you:
- Create plausible understandings
- Test them out with other people
- Then refine or abandon.

You might say 'yeah I do that every freakin' day!' And well you might for you may be a knowledge worker.

We got through that infection crisis at the hospital with no casualties, but it was such a tense and challenging time that the crisis of it leaves some psychological scar tissue on all who were impacted.

A lot like improv

To contrast the drama of a public crisis, it's been super fun, insightful and challenging to learn, practice and perform with the improv troupe in Melbourne, *Impro Melbourne*.

In many cities across the world, improv troupes get together and perform live by giving deliriously wonderful and deeply touching performances. Made up on the spot.

I wrote about them in my previous book *'Create Change'* and how some audiences on the way out after a great performance say 'gee I'm coming back tomorrow night to see it again'. Except it won't be the same tomorrow night. We don't know what it will be tomorrow night.

Improvisers work from a set of principles. That's how they make that stuff up.

It's a little like that in making sense. No hard and fast rules, but some principles to abide by and take into account when you're in it.

Weick says sense making is like being thrown into the unknown. Improv is like that. You don't know what people will say next!

Weick's suggestion that you're looking for answers to the key question of 'What's the story?' is just like improv. You're driven to create and craft a story right there on stage with other performers and you don't know what they're going to do or say next but you're gonna make something out of it.

And you just have to keep playing. Unless the performance is really shit. Then the judges blow a horn and everyone is relieved and the performers cheer with joy and leave the stage. That bit is over for everyone and we can start 'again'.

Improvisers have to kind of handle what's happening and simultaneously contribute to the scene or the story that's unfolding. A little like patting your head and rubbing your stomach. A mix of capabilities, hey?

Ancona says leaders need self-awareness and emotional intelligence and be able to deal with cognitive complexity. Hell yeah! And some flexibility as well. To be able to handle the **what is** and the **what if**. And play well with others.

No wonder this making sense is a serious leadership capability.

No wonder not many people are helping us learn how to do it; we're struggling with it ourselves, let alone helping us learn how to make sense.

Cynefin and Cognitive Edge

You can't mention, think or talk about sense making or sensemaking or making sense, without reference to Dave Snowden and Cognitive Edge.

The 2007 Harvard Business Review article by Snowden and Mary Boone is often quoted, cited, read and re-read. It really is a pocket guide to sense making and a must as a discussion starter and entrée to the topic for a workplace, team or project. It's a winner.

There is also plenty of Cognitive Edge videos, blogs and articles which are gems. Each offers a new insight, opportunities for deeper learning and thinking and prompts for application. Yes, I'm a fan!

It's Cynefin (sort of pronounced kin-evan) and it's a Welsh term. While it doesn't translate directly in English it has some common meanings of 'habitat' or 'place'. It means a place of multiple belongings.

When you think of your own life, you've been impacted and influenced by so many different places, things, people, cultures. In essence the Cynefin tool helps you look at things from different angles. That's what perspective is all about. And too often, arguments, disagreements and slow progress happen because we either can't see another perspective or aren't even aware that another viewpoint or angle exists. We're so hardwired and tied in to our preferred styles (from our multiple belongings) that they cause us to not truly 'see'.

So Cynefin is a framework. If you can see where you are, you can make sense and get on and act. Decisions will be better and you'll be in progress and motion.

The Cynefin framework evolved and developed over the years and other names such as Cynthia Kurtz and Mary Boone need to be footnoted to it's evolution.

The Cynefin Framework from Dave Snowden & Cognitive Edge

Visual by Lynne Cazaly

In short, there are different types of systems and when you're in a different system or situation, you might need a different approach to thinking and making decisions and acting.

In a ScrumSense article this quote about Cynefin:

"In a categorisation model, the framework precedes the data. This is good for exploitation but not exploration. In a sense-making model the data precedes the framework, making it good for exploration."

This is what I love; the idea that you can go exploring, explore the thinking, the information, the data and the situation.

So the types of systems that Cynefin quotes are:

- Ordered: Simple and Complication
- Complex
- Chaotic

That's five 'domains' in all: Simple, Complicated, Complex, Chaotic and Disorder (you'll see that one sitting in the centre of the image).

Go to any leadership or innovation conference and one of the presenters is sure to whip out a quote by Einstein; perhaps this one: *"We can't solve problems by using the same kind of thinking we used when we created them." – Albert Einstein*

And if you apply that to making sense of things, then yes, we do need to have a go at looking from a different angle, perspective, view or position. You may have to suspend your own routine, habitual thinking.

You may need to, as social researcher Hugh Mackay says, 'listen' and often we don't listen to others particularly well because we're fearful of how their views and thinking might change us. That's a pretty scary situation for our lizard brain; "Oh shit! I might be changed if I listen to this!"

So here's the thing about Cynefin:

Simple

The **simple** domain shows we're in an ordered system. We can readily find a relationship between cause and effect. So the advice here is to Sense, Categorise, Respond. That means see what's coming in, make it fit to some categories you've set up and then work out what you're going to do.

Complicated

In the **complicated** domain, there is an ordered system and a right answer and yes, another connection or relationship between cause and effect... but it's not as obvious to us. We've got to think some more, perhaps apply some expert knowledge. That means we see what's coming in, investigate or analyse... then respond and decide what to do.

Complex

In the **complex** domain, ooooh, we have unorder. You can only work out the relationship between cause and effect by looking backwards, seeing it as it has already occurred. That means we need to be more open to experimenting, trying things out and then we can make sense of it.

Snowden refers to 'safe to fail' experiments, and when he's presented at conferences on software development, that's been a 'hallelujah' from the delegates: you want the go-ahead to try things out and see what works. Just applying what someone else says is 'best practice' isn't going to work.

Experimentation is key. Turn up the parts that worked, dial down the parts that didn't. In that way we probe, experiment and sense for what worked and what didn't, then respond with a decision to ramp things up or dial them down.

Chaotic

Then the **chaotic** domain; there is no cause and effect relationship identified. It's chaos! So let's get stable, quick! In that way we act to stabilize, then sense, looking for failures and successes and then respond by deciding what to do next.

And what of **disorder**? It's when you don't know what space you're in so you tend to go for your own favourite approach or head off to your comfort zone.

When you need to apply a sensemaking approach, check out where you might be heading with the Cyenfin framework. Do you go for the best practice or expert response, or do you go probing, or is experimenting the approach?

Every situation is different and so we need different responses. The U in VUCA is uncertainty. We've got to flex and adapt and shift and be responsive.

Learning to lead and adapt

Making sense can bring so many other domains into the story of sense making. There's crossover and synergy – buzzwords not intended, but there really is synergy! It's about making connections, plausible ones. So it's plausible that almost any field could find itself connected to the work of sense making.

That's part of the improvisation of sensemaking. There's uncertainty anyway, so let's add in a bit more and see if we can make something of it.

In the making is learning. There's such a big connection between sense making and agility, learning, improving and adapting.

In *Leadership Agility: Five Levels of Mastery for Anticipating and Initiating Change* by William B. Joiner, Stephen A. Josephs, there are many agile connections.

They say that agile leaders, responsive and adaptive leaders

> "are more strategic in their thinking, more collaborative, more proactive in seeking feedback, more effective in resolving conflicts, more active in developing subordinates, and more likely to redefine problems to capitalize on the connections between them."

They suggest,

> "Context-setting agility improves your ability to scan your environment, frame the initiatives you need to take, and clarify the outcomes you need to achieve."

…and that you try on frames of reference that differ from your own. Further, they say, "you temporarily drop your own frame and adopt one with alternative assumptions and priorities long enough to understand what a situation looks like from a new perspective. This capacity, which allows you to import ideas from other frames of reference into your own, also makes you a more creative thinker."

To wrap this up, Joiner and Josephs say "you see that diametrically opposed ideas are related to one another along a continuum with many shades of gray between them."

How many Shades of Grey? Four, twelve, fifty?

"Context-setting agility improves your ability to scan your environment, frame the initiatives you need to take, and clarify the outcomes you need to achieve."

From 'Leadership Agility:
Five Levels of Mastery for Anticipating
and Initiating Change

- William B. Joiner, Stephen A. Josephs,

It's about a map

Making sense is about coming up with a plausible understanding - a map - of a shifting world. Then we test the map with others - whether through collecting data or acting or conversation, then we refine or abandon the map, depending on how credible it is.

Sensemaking helps you grasp what's going on.

Ancona suggests it involves the three stages of:
- explore the wider system
- create a map of that system
- act in the system.

Sense making and making sense is about this map. It's the step in between the thinking and the acting. Maps guide us, show us where, what and some steps for how. If we don't know where we're going, it's the GPS in our cars or on our smart phones and devices that gives us some calm among high levels of uncertainty.

Applying a mapping approach to the world of work is what helps people feel like they are working 'on the same page'.

Think about heading off on a journey, holiday or road trip. Do you just drive? Perhaps. A day trip - 'let's see where we end up.' Lovely. At work, it's an opportunity for creativity, innovation and experimentation.

But it may not be possible every working day.

When you don't know the road ahead on the journey or the day trip you're on, a quick check of the map shows the conditions and traffic and shows landmarks, features and services.

In the dusty Australian outback deserts and remote areas my husband Michael and I travel, the use of contemporary and up to date mapping is critical. As we travel across deserts, sand dunes have been mapped - and while they change from season to season - nothing seems to remove them totally from the map, or the territory.

So we'll be looking at a map, driving across the desert, checking the map again, keep on driving... see a town on the map... keep driving.... and we often see things that have moved, changed or shifted compared to the map.

It's great to see the Hema Map team out on 4WD and remote tracks keeping maps up to date as new features and changes to the landscape occur. Remote and isolated travellers need those maps. Just like workers in unknown situations need some type of reference, guide or bigger picture.

You can be sure this is not about being 100% sure! We're not going to get it totally correct or right. We won't ever be 'done' with it or correct and finished and right when making sense. It's an ongoing thing. It will get more detailed, deeper, more insightful, more helpful.

If it's about maps, it's relieving to know we don't all have to be cartographers. You know what it's like; you're on a road trip with friends and maybe one of you knows where you're

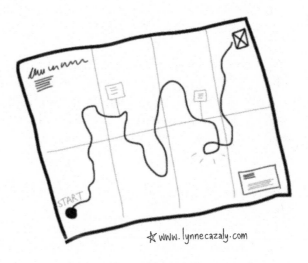

★ www.lynnecazaly.com

going. The driver. The others may say 'where are we going?' or 'when do we get there?'

With a current day GPS you've got the map played out in front of you. For the relief of passengers on board, you can show the route you're going to take and they can see where they are.

This is why the flight path or aerial maps on board planes are so popular - along with the movies! People want to know where they are, where they're going, when we'll get there, how fast we're going.

It's a great anxiety alleviator. The same thing applies at work.

When people are worried, uncertain, unsure, stressed, distressed, freaked out - show them the way. Show them where they are now, show them where you're going. Use a map to help them make sense.

And relax about the map-ness of this. There is no one right answer. While you may choose a map to get from here to Copenhagen, you can of course take many different routes. You can fly, drive, ferry, cycle, and take different routes. This is a map; we can go many different ways. And our journey may change along the way. Think of roadworks, diversions or routes that are out of action.

Or as some friends who were travelling in Japan and dutifully following the Japanese language directions on the GPS found out; the road they were happily travelling on, all bright shiny and new, was unknown to the GPS. The GPS kept assuring them in Japanese they were 'in the water' and 'get out of the water'.

Bridge over waters, no trouble here at all. The reality was ahead of the map.

And Ancona says that plausibility rather than accuracy is the go. You want to get people interested, engaged, willing to join

Making Sense - Lynne Cazaly

in the conversation and start making sense so give it your best go.

Leaders need this sensemaking capability because the more sense we can make, the clearer things are, the better and more smoothly our interactions with others be. We'll be better collaborators and engagers and team players and co-creators. Hooray!

Darshan Desai in *'The Art of Sensemaking: The Right Question at the Right Time'* says that as we explore the information and move from things being messy to getting some clarity, we move towards a 'workable certainty'. We might not be able to fully grasp all of the details, because we're in the process of sense making, but we've got to a point where it's 'workable'.

The emphasis here is on asking questions; if you just listen you won't get to the heart of what you're listening to. This reinforces the 'conversation' aspect of sense making. There's an exchange, a sharing and a 'two way' of information.

Talking.
Listening.
Thinking.
Mapping.
Making of sense.

"So thinking—truly focused thinking, which includes mental activities such as observing, remembering, wondering, imagining, inquiring, interpreting, evaluating, judging, identifying, supposing, composing, comparing, analyzing, calculating, and even metacognition (thinking about thinking)—is hard work."

From 'Think Better: An Innovator's Guide to Productive Thinking'
- Tim Hurson

think

map

act

"Intersection thinking is a method for creating overlap between seemingly disconnected ideas in order to generate new ideas, directions and strategies for powering your own success."

From 'Non-Obvious: How to Think Different, Curate Ideas & Predict The Future'

- Rohit Bhargava

All talk ... it's not enough

When you watch a team member or a leader in a meeting, doing their best to make sense of things, here's what they're too often doing:

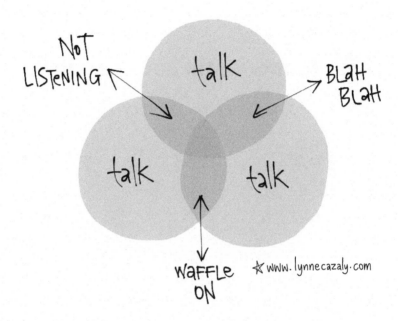

It's all talk. They're talking and talking and talking and more talking. There's rarely a process set out that the meeting or conversation is following. And while I support the opportunity to get things off your chest or just let it flow, there's a point where that's not helpful.

You've got to have some structure, some way of seeing what you're thinking and talking about, so you know what you can act on.

The same happens if you're just thinking, thinking, thinking and not sharing it or not acting on what you're thinking.

I believe we have a preference, for either a:

- Talk track, or
- Thought track.

Our preference goes to either thinking about things first, or talking about things first. Then when we think we're done, we act.

Think & act ... still not enough

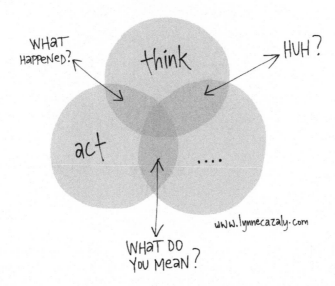

At its basics, making sense is doing these two things; thinking and acting. You think about stuff and then you act on it.

But I think there's more to it; thinking and acting isn't quite enough. I think there's this 'map' section that sits between the thinking and acting.

Making Sense - Lynne Cazaly

THINK, MAP, ACT

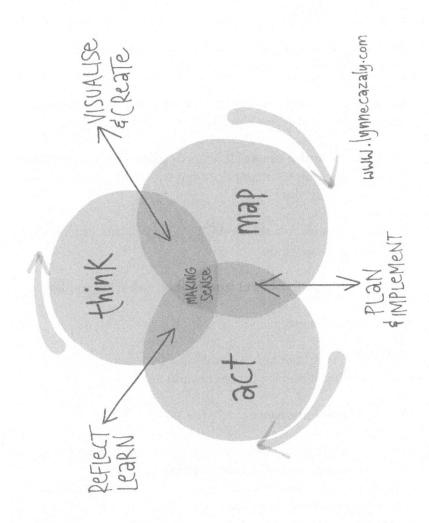

Now we're getting there! This is it!

THINK. MAP. ACT.

First, there is **THINK**.

We engage in thinking. This is the opportunity for us imagine, picture, envision... to **visualize and create**.

We can then bring that imagining or envisioning a version or prototype into reality, we can **MAP** our thinking and ideas.

This helps us **make sense**. It helps us **plan and implement** and work out what we might do, what we can do, what we will do... together or alone.

Because of this we are able to **ACT**. We put it into practice, we commit to action, we do.

Then we are able to **reflect and learn** from what we did.

This is making sense.

And we can continue on. Now we have done something, we can learn from it and we can go around again.

We can **think** some more.

We go around again. We know more now. Let's **map** it out again, **act** again, and start over to **think** again.

This is making sense. It is ongoing, it's cyclical, it is different every time because we have thought, mapped and acted, and now we know more. We will think differently, see it differently and be able to act differently because our knowledge and experience has shifted and changed. We have new things to make sense of.

THINK

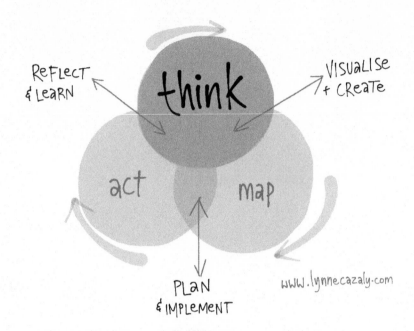

REFLECT & LEARN

VISUALISE + CREATE

think

act

map

PLAN & IMPLEMENT

www.lynnecazaly.com

Making Sense - Lynne Cazaly

Humans and their big biases

When it comes to thinking, we have this little problem... well a big one actually; you can't see it, but it's there. We all have it. And it's getting in the way of so many things. In fact it's not just one thing; it's lots.

It's called Cognitive Bias.

In short, we all reckon we're balanced, clear thinking and logical individuals. We try hard to be and reckon we're quite good at it. But umm, well, I've got to tell you this, we're not as good as we think we are. We are super, super biased. And cognitive bias is the big mofo bias of them all. Aaaarrghhh!

As your day goes on today you'll be taking in information and working things out and problem solving and sprouting forth your views and ideas and thinking. And you'll think you're doing an awesome job at it. But in our efforts to be awesome, we're also trying to simplify things.

You know, Leonardo Da Vinci said 'simplicity is the ultimate sophistication' so we're all trying to be very Da Vinci and keep it simple. We're only trying to get shit done after all.

But biases get in the way and can cause us to make silly mistakes or errors. We all have them. No need to feel guilt, shame or revisit Brene Brown's work on vulnerability for this one. In fact, just accept it. We're biased. It's not evil either. These are mighty helpful survival tools. They've been responsible for helping us make some most awesome discoveries across the history of the world.

Cognitive biases are rooted. They're rooted in how we think. You know when a computer app or software crashes or has an error message? That's all a cognitive bias is, a little processing error that kicks in because there's a problem (not major, relax...)

a problem with say, our memory, or our attention or some other little things our brain is busy doing.

There are so many of these biases. Here's just a few to watch out for in the sensemaking domain or space:

Confirmation Bias

Here's where you favour some information out there that confirms what you previously believed. You find and seek out proof and evidence and facts and more data and reasonings and more and more 'stuff' to back up what you think and believe to be true.

And all of those other views and facts and data that contradict your view... yeah, they get trashed. Not needed because they don't confirm what you already believe. Watch out for this one. Pops up constantly throughout the day!

Halo Effect

This bias is when your overall impression of someone influences how you feel about them and their character. It's like when you hear someone report back on another person they've just met.

They'll say 'oh she was so nice' or 'he was so calm' or 'she was so organised', and that influences your evaluations of other aspects of their personality and character.

'She's so nice AND she's an awesome business woman' or 'He's so calm AND he's a brilliant mentor'.

In the words of Beyoncé,
Everywhere I'm looking now
I'm surrounded by your embrace
Baby, I can see your halo
You know you're my saving grace

In fact the Halo effect works well with celebrities. We think they're <insert long list of positive characteristics of your favourite celebrity or actor or musician>. When they're attractive or sing well, we think they're also smart, funny, generous. And Beyoncé probably is. That's the Halo Effect working on me.

Self-Serving Bias

Here's when we give applause for the successes we're involved with and blame others for the failures. It's all about what *we* did that made something successful; it's all about how *they* stuffed up when it fails. Think of it like this: 'I succeeded because of my awesome traits, characteristics and talent. It didn't work or it failed because they stuffed up, didn't send something in on time or were totally incompetent'. Yeah, it was nothing that I did.

I remember completing my final year at high school and using a self-serving bias. I did super well on the English exam; that's because I studied hard, have natural talents in this area and <other awesome thought about myself>.

However, Legal Studies? Oh you wouldn't believe that exam. The examiner, who was watching over us in our local church hall where we sat our exams, was so bored each day she chose interesting tasks to occupy herself while she observed us. On day one she glued back together the Bibles that had been falling apart, pages had become unglued. That wasn't noisy or visually disturbing, but it was smelly. Smelly glue.

On day two, get this... she did her ironing. HER IRONING! The examiner brought in her ironing board, set it up and proceeded to iron hers (and her neighbour's laundry).

That noisy steaming iron hissed and spat and the ironing board creaked and moaned. All through my Legal Studies exam. As a result of her ironing and the ridiculous distraction it caused, I only got 52% for my exam. I knew the information, but it was *her* fault that *she* was distracting and not creating a perfect examination and testing environment.

That is a self-serving bias right there! It wasn't my lack of preparation or study or completion of appropriate exam pre-work; no it was her and that hissing iron!

Attentional Bias

This bias kicks in in times of uncertainty, group work and decision-making. We often jump to our decision, thinking we've taken a bunch of options, information and alternatives into account. But, ooops, we haven't. We're biased with our attention. We get hyper focused. Looking at the 'good', not seeing the 'bad' or even the 'other' information.

There are so many more cognitive biases; watch out for them taking over, kicking in or working on you while you're trying to make sense of complexity.

How we think

I enjoyed Daniel Kahneman's book *'Thinking Fast and Slow'* and absorbing all the research, information and results on how our brains deal with the daily tasks, information processing and problem solving that continues to come at us at a great rate of speed.

Peter Senge's classic leadership read *'The Fifth Discipline'* is also a bright insight to how we think. It dives into systems thinking and a systems perspective. He speaks of the programming and conditioning we've had, over and over again; no wonder our 'mental models' kick in and quickly give us an answer – it's from years of repetitive thinking and problem solving.

Even his Archetype 1 and Archetype 2 give us some guidance on how we can be limited in our thinking, reinforcing an existing process (Archetype 1). And then we can be reinforcing the loop or process rather than thinking about changing how we think (Archetype 2).

Senge says that what 'we carry in our heads are images, assumptions and stories'… and many of these are deeply ingrained paradigms. Assumptions, limitations and biases all play tricks on us to keep us thinking how we have always been thinking.

Our mental models help us see, shape, categorise and organize information. Breaking that model? Well that's going to be hard work. Senge's comment that it's our mental models that determine the sense we make of information, not what information we have... is gold.

When I'm working with teams and groups, it's a joyous thing to get to the point when the team realizes it's *their* thinking that is shaping what they're talking about. It's their mental models that will decide what they do. And to challenge them to change their mental models... well that's a whole other workshop in itself!

Peter Senge encourages us to bring our mental models into full view. He says we should 'surface, expose and bring into conversation' the things we're thinking about. Yay! Let's do that. I'm in!

And then when we *do* put our thinking out there, explain how you came to think that; add in the assumptions you're making, the questions you still have and what you'd like from others in (and out of) the room.

Above all, Senge says all we have are 'assumptions, never truths'. It reminded me again of Hugh Mackay's *'Why don't people listen'* book and his description that we see the world through our 'cages'; the structures of our thinking, beliefs, values and experiences.

They're our mental models.

We all have them. We all look and think through them. And you can argue and debate someone else's view for hours –

sometimes I think that's what most workplace meetings are about. Too much talking, too little sensemaking.

In that way we'll be learning not just restating, LOUDER!
Take some reflection time. Listen to yourself.

In a leadership workshop I facilitated recently I encouraged the senior leadership team to audio record themselves for the coming week. This was so they could listen back to how they sounded, what they said, how they said it.

Several of them noticed how often that spoke LOUDER, repeating similar words and phrases when people disagreed or didn't understand what they'd said. They were saying the same thing all over again, just L-O-U-D-E-R as if the person they were with hadn't heard.

Talk about a learning opportunity! Repeating? It's just repeating. It's not finding a common ground or a clarity or worse, it's not about making sense. And when you're in a leadership role, you've got to help people make sense.

It starts with listening

There is no making sense without listening. You can't make sense for yourself or others without some good time spent in still, shutupness, peace and quiet.

Silent.

That means listening to the other person, not working out your response.

Just listening and asking yourself 'what do they mean? What is this about?'

Most of us would know how it feels to **not** be listened to. For someone to give you great advice, to tell you what to do. They think they're doing well by giving you a solution to ease your pain. But perhaps all we want is to be listened to. To be heard. To be understood. To be validated that what we think or feel is normal, sensible, logical or understandable.

That is it. That is the big, big thing about making sense, about having empathy. It's just that we want to know we're ok and we can carry on and we're doing the best we can. But instead of helping and giving people that short moment of 'yes you're ok', we jump in with our contrasting views, our arguments and defenses, our debates and 'rights' and opinions.

It's a shame. It adds to the non sense.

As soon as you stop, listen, really listen, reflect back and give people a sense of their sense, you make huge inroads. You make wonderful progress in trust, collaboration and productivity. The environment around you is eased and safe and you're on the freeway for producing good work, communicating well and ticking things off.

Too bad more leaders don't pause more often, listen better and wait before they respond and bat back with their defense or justifications. We'd all achieve more, the workplace would be a sweeter place to work and we'd have less problems with turnover, low trust, disengagement and other contemporary problems that leaders at all levels are experiencing.

I'm not suggesting it's the ONLY thing that contributes to low levels of trust or other workplace and people issues, but it's a big one. A big one.

You need only see how people behave when they *are* listened to, to see. Most people don't get to see this because ... they don't really listen to people.

I think sensemaking helps people hear each other. And that makes sensemaking a generous and helpful gift.

It could get messy around here

Earlier when I wrote about knowledge workers, I was reminded of how many knowledge workers have cluttered desks and floors … and they (umm, that would be me) can easily find whatever piece of information they need from the piles of papers around their feet, on their shelves and in corners.

In a presentation by Divya Mishra on knowledge workers, I was reminded that they can also be disrupted when changes are made to what seems to be a messy pile. Just ask one of them if they've had a friend, family member or visitor clean up for them. What might look like chaos to others is organized muddle. They know where things are; and when it's been cleaned up the whole layout has changed.

Knowledge workers use the physical space of a desk or floor as a holding pattern for their ideas and inputs. It's like what an air traffic controller does with planes in the sky; if the airport isn't ready for them to land, they fly about in a holding pattern or they slow down and apply speed restrictions. The air traffic controller waits until the weather clears or a slot becomes available for the plane to land.

For knowledge workers, they often can't decide how they're going to use or 'land' the information. This can also be the case in book writing; lots of inputs but how do you want to use them?

Filing information seems foolish. You can't put it away and out of sight! It might be needed later. Or sooner.

And then when there's been a break – think a coffee break or lunch or worse, an interruption – the flow has been altered and you might hear them say… 'now where was I?'

Looking at that messy map of papers, workbooks, sketches, articles or print outs can be the immediate cue that knowledge workers need.

So if things start to get messy with sensemaking, relax, take it easy and don't clean up... yet. It could be just how some of us like it and just how it needs to be.

I remember when a friend Shaun came to visit. He walked into my home office one day and said 'How do you work in here?' Shaun is an ordered and organised kind of guy. I'm not. I'm in chaos, looking for clarity, making sense of things. I need the mess. I know where stuff is, but it's the happy accidents, the way that Post-it Note randomly stuck to something totally unrelated that helped me get to some other areas of sense making ... that just would not have happened had it been all tidy and ordered like Shaun's office.

I envy Shaun's office. I tidy up occasionally wanting it all to look like Shaun's office. It barely lasts a day. In fact, it never looks like Shaun's office. Hey there Shaun ☺

On the following pages are 10 thinking tools for making sense.

Go.
Think.
Make sense.

10 Thinking Tools for Making Sense

"Something happens when people tell each other the truth. When we visualize reality, we become much more accountable and supportive of each other in our behaviors and actions to lead the business."

From The Art of Engagement: Bridging the Gap Between People and Possibilities

- Jim Haudan

10 Thinking Tools for Making Sense

These are ten steps (and use them in any order) to work through when facilitating groups and working with teams, to help them make sense of things, helping them get practical. It takes you into the information, but it also brings you out.

Use them in meetings, workshops and conversations. Use them to keep your thinking going. Most of all, use them to map out thinking so you can make sense and visualize what's going on.

1. Clarify the context
Why are we doing this, talking this or working on this? Set a big picture reason 'why' and the context will be clear.

Too often conversations are had at this high level yet we don't realise we're debating it, or worse, we agree on it but we haven't made it clear we agree.

Great mediators and conflict negotiators know that if they get high-level agreement, they're already part of the way there.
The same applies to making sense of stuff.

If you know what lens or viewfinder you're looking through, things can be viewed with that in mind. Don't make it explicit and you'll be darting all over the context looking for it!

What's the why, why are we here, what are we trying to do - big picture. Google Earth/Maps view, big big picture. Stop the detail drillers. Not required right now.

Clarify

2. Traverse the breadth

Map out what the scope of this thing could be. It's not where you're going right now, but by identifying how broad this thing is, helps flag where people might get caught up.

Once you've named or identified the breadth, you can draw people in to focus on parts of 'now'.

When tangents are taken by people in the team trying to make sense, you can flag where they are on the breadth. It's just like taking a trip from London to Paris. That is bigger context. The breadth is, well, London.... to Paris. You could map it out. You could draw a line, at one end London, at the other, Paris. We could get there in many different ways, and that's something to discuss, decide and agree on.

Let's say we're on the train, the Eurostar. Along the way, along the breadth is that part out of London when it gets all green luscious and countryside, there's the part where you're going into the tunnel, then there's the tunnel, then coming up the other side, then countryside, towns, outer city, Paris, station!

That's the breadth.

Same with your topics, discussion, planning and work.

There is breadth. Which bit are you going to do?

Traverse

Making Sense - Lynne Cazaly

3. Explore the depths

Now where are you going to dive down? If you're on that train from London to Paris, are you getting off at one of the stations along the path? Or heading to the end of the line?

Choose where you'll deep dive and what you'll deep dive on.

Stop the scattering and diluted time wasting (non-sense creating) when you're darting from here to there, back to that, over to there and then back again. It's hard work. It takes brain-processing energy to keep making sense of where we are again and again.

It's just like how a GPS freaks out a little when you don't follow the suggested route. You know when it displays the 'recalculating route' or other type of message. You're not going there, so maybe you want to go this way. The GPS is in effect saying 'you haven't followed what I've said, so let me find another way for you.'

Same goes with exploring the depths.

You're on this path now; which path are you going to take from here?

4. Deduce the meaning

As you go into the depth on this topic or thing, try and get to meaning, to understanding and comprehension as quickly as possible.

Dan Roam in his book *The Back of the Napkin* talks about the one who gets to meaning the quickest is the winner. The one who finds the solution is the winner - 'the one' being a team as well as a lone, sole individual!

The sooner you can capture and represent the meaning of things - as you progress - the better progress, the better sense you'll make. You can take it step by step, make some meaning, and move on throughout the process.

Help people understand. Get to the meaning of what this is about.

Go high enough into context so that it's:
- relevant to your project or piece of work,
- connected directly to the context you set earlier and
- making sense for you and those involved.

Aaaaah, but how do you know if it's making sense to them? Ask.

Ask not 'Is this making sense?' or 'Does this make sense?' Both of those questions are tragic closed yes/no answers.

Ask 'How is this making sense for you?' or 'What sense is this making right now? or 'What sense are you getting from this?' All of these are open questions, inviting people to make a summary, a potted history of the meaning they're getting now.

Deduce

5. Distill the essence

Of everything covered, discussed, collated, created, what's the essence of that, up to now? This is a great progress summary or a snapshot of where you are.

I think when you and a team or group can tick off and make sense of chunks of discussion or progress, you're truly making sense. We can close off that part and then be able to move on to the next part, topic, talk, content or work. If it's left open, unresolved, unanswered, unsummarised, you can't get forward momentum. You'll keep looping back here until it's done.

The film *Looper* starring Emily Blunt showed a loop in a loop situation of people coming back to life, to the past, to wipe others off the planet. We're not getting that evil in the future of work thank you! But it's a great example of how you can lose track of now, the past, the present, the future because of broken loops.

You may have seen or heard a 'looper' in a meeting or workshop – someone who doesn't move on to new topics or get to decisions because they're caught up in an infinity loop. It's a loop of non-sense because they're trying to make sense. That's not a bad thing. They just need some assistance to move on and close a loop. They're not able to resolve this piece and so they stay there or regress there until it's closed up. It's the leader or facilitator's job to do this. It's the sense maker's job. The person who elegantly and succinctly summarises what this is about. It makes sense and it validates what that person was revisiting. The sense maker may not bring it all down to a single word – that can be open to semantics - but they may choose a number of words, a phrase or two, using the words people have used.

Distilling and reflection is a delightful sense making tool because it helps people hear each other.

Distill

6. Connect the parts

You know when you meet someone and you realise you both know someone else, a third person? Maybe you're looking on LinkedIn or other social media and you connect with someone and then you see who else they know. You can end up knowing a lot of people that you didn't realise you both know!

Other times there is no connection. Just a random matching - or at least it can feel like that!

The same with information and making sense. There can be disparate pieces all spinning on their own axis but not until you connect them does it make sense for people. Often we're so busy holding one point or one piece of information in our head that being able to connect seemingly unrelated pieces is just too hard right now. You can't go there. You're busy handling this, here now.

Help people make sense by connecting things for them. Help them see how things are related. Be explicit. Say it. And say it again.

As Matt Church of Thought Leaders Global says: 'they're not listening, they don't care and you don't matter'. A little disheartening? No. It's the truth. We're focused on things important to us. What your project or piece of work is doing has got nothing to do with me, until you make it have something to do with me. 'Connecting the dots' is a classic expression or idiom and refers to how people make connections between different pieces of information.

Connect related parts ... and unrelated parts. Say if they're unrelated; and say how they are related. We'll be able to hold this information and compartmentalise it all the better when we connect the parts and make sense.

Connect

7. Relate to others

Part of the sense making process is about connecting and relating … to people. People. The humans that do the doing, think the thinking and make and sense the sense making.

Be sure to relate your thinking, working and creating to the people involved in it and with it.

Put them in the picture, physically. Name them, place them, locate them and identify them so we know who is where, who is that, where they are and what they are doing.

When you put people in the picture, when you relate the topics and content to people, you humanise it. You make even more sense of it.

Sense making is a human thing. This is the number one capability for the future of work.

Show me where the humans are and how they're connected to this. Relate your thinking, your message and your ideas to people… to others, as well as your self.

Relate

8. Transfer the message

There's a saying that a problem shared is a problem halved.

The same with making sense.

A key problem in ambiguity and complexity is the lack of sharing of information. Sure that information is sitting somewhere, in a digital form, in a file or folder on a desktop or shared drive or the cloud. But it's not graspable. People struggle to put their hands on it. They'll use that phrasing: 'let me get hold of that report and I'll send it through to you...' or 'we've got to get to grips with this...'

Get on the front foot and transfer the information, the sense and the message to others. When you've distilled it - make it able to be shared, worked on further and co-created by others.

Viral messages are viral because they're so easily shared.

Make sense more sensible and sense-able by sharing and transferring it to others.

When businesses identify champions of change, change makers or centres of influence, they're looking for the people who can take a message and get it on out there to build, influence and shape change.

Package your point so it's an easy and tasty takeaway.

Transfer

9. Move to act

Conversations and work without implementation or action is non-sense.

It's crazy, time wasting, anti productive and foolish irresponsible waste.

With many meetings, teams, business units and individuals being measured on what is performed – key performance indicators or KPIs - what are you ***doing*** about it?

Once you've made sense of something, how are you sharing it, inspiring others to act and mapping out some possible actions?

Do something with it... or you'll be back in the same room talking about the same stuff next week and you'll be no further advanced. That's non-sense. It's wasteful of time, resources and energy.

Talk, sure. Think, absolutely. But then you must act... in that way you'll build more sense and be able to adjust your actions.

What can you act on?

10. Extend the thinking
Go again.

Think, map, act is a brilliant three step dance of sorts. You just keep on going. Waltzing around. Or was it a polka or the Pride of Erin!

As you launch into the next phase of thinking, you will know more from your actions.

The information has changed, your knowledge and awareness has shifted. It's a different place and space than it was.

You will know more; they will know more; you will have information available to you that you didn't have when you began, so go again.

Keep making sense. Go again.

Extend

MAP

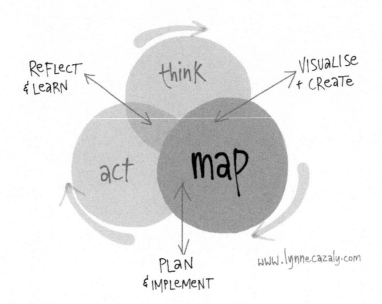

REFLECT & LEARN

think

VISUALISE + CREATE

act

map

PLAN & IMPLEMENT

www.lynnecazaly.com

Maps and Cartography

Static maps of two dimensional things – locations, objects, the universe, stars and planets – have a history as old as time. More recently, three dimensional and interactive maps have given us more knowledge, awareness, access and opportunity.

We're able to depict so much information, so much detail on a map, thanks to the use of symbols and icons that replace the need for many words.

And with the rise of digital mapping on our phones and devices, I think we're breeding a new generation of map lovin' people.

☆ www.lynnecazaly.com

"A map does not just chart, it unlocks and formulates meaning; it forms bridges between here and there, between disparate ideas that we did not know were previously connected."

From The Selected Works of T.S. Spivet

- Reif Larsen

Maps and visual stories

There's no doubt that stories are in vogue; they've always been. Leadership and business storytelling is hot right now. Storytelling workshops are on workplace training agendas and leaders are using stories as a way to engage, inspire and lead people in teams.

Storytelling thought leaders Gabrielle Dolan and Yamini Naidu in their book *Hooked* share the elements of success for stories.

They needn't be lengthy tomes. They can be short, 90 seconds or so and the more truthful and individual or personal, the better.

So with the rise of stories, comes an opportunity: to bring stories to life in a visual format. To map a story.

You can combine the power of the emotional word with the added power of a visual image.

Come to think of it, this is what movies are. This is what fiction writing it.

Stories.
With pictures - whether constructed by a film crew and director or written by an author, creating mental mind pictures to be transferred from their typing fingers, to the page, to your mind.

Sketch for Sense

If you've read any of my previous work or seen the visuals throughout this book or at my website, you'll notice they're handcrafted and it's a thing of mine.

I have no formal artistic training. And I'm no huge art lover or art knower. So I'm not coming at this from art. I'm coming at this from clarity, knowing, sense making and communicating outcomes… in a real and human way.

So I believe one of the shortest routes to making sense of something is to sketch for sense. It's not in stone. It's not final. It's very low-fi in fact. It's an early iteration. A first draft. A first crack at it. It's your thinking on show. Just some of your thoughts - not everything you know, nor everything you think on this topic. It's a first pass.

It's something to work with, work on, share with others, begin to craft, edit and shape and a collection or curation of thoughts, as of now. Things might change. Or they might not.

But sketching for sense is the grown up thing to do. It will be quick, clear, collaborative, communicative, responsible and responsive. And once you've got your thoughts out there you can get to work on them, with others or alone.

So here are ten things you can do when you sketch for sense:
1. Jot
2. Explore
3. Refine
4. Develop
5. Refer
6. Record
7. Collect
8. Archive
9. Focus
10. Expand

Everyone should be doing it

Sketching is not just for artists. This is a human communication capability and skill. We make sense of plenty of things in life; let's extend this capability to every corner of the workplace, every conversation, every interaction, ever process, plan and priority. Where is the sense making in it? It's not reserved for the 'talented one' in the team. It's not reserved for the person who has an interest in cartooning! It's something everyone should be doing. At all levels, at all capabilities and cultures. No matter your interest or expertise, capability or talent, you already make sense of things; lets extend that to all elements of work.

It's not about art or drawing

Yes, this thing again about art. Making sense and using visuals or sketches for that is not about drawing or art capability. You can use the visual elements to deduce, plan, communicate, map, think, but it's not about how capable an artist you are or how well you can sketch out a picture of a dolphin leaping through the air. It's about the thinking, the process, the craft and the making of. Not the thing itself.

It's about thinking

Making sense and sketching is what you think about it, what's related to it, what's next door, what's different and what's similar. It's your thinking on how this piece connects to that, how it is related and how it isn't. It's not the drawing that matters; it's the thinking, the talking, the mapping out and the process of getting to sense making. That's what matters.

A 'how to' model for maps and sense making

When I'm working with teams and individuals teaching and training in my workshops on visual thinking, visual facilitating, sense making and listening, this is my four step, "get me out of trouble and get me into the zone" model.

1. Prepare

No craftsman or expert starts work on their craft without getting ready. Same for the sense maker. Get your shit together. Get your tools ready, your materials at hand and be prepared for not knowing.

2. Listen

Don't write or draw a thing. Just listen. Chill out. Relax. Listen. What are they saying? What's this about? No, what's it REALLY about? Have they even made a point yet? Or are they building up to it? Is this background research and data? Have they made their epiphany known yet? Are they trying to convince you of something? What's that? What's their main message, point or pitch? What is that? Keep listening. Is there a theme emerging. What is it? Have there been any metaphors or stories shared? What are they? How do they connect?

3. Capture

Write it down. Use familiar, simple, clear words. Don't worry about the drawing aspect of it. Just get down the essence; what's this about? Capture only what's relevant; that's why context is important in sensemaking and the mapping and visualizing of it.

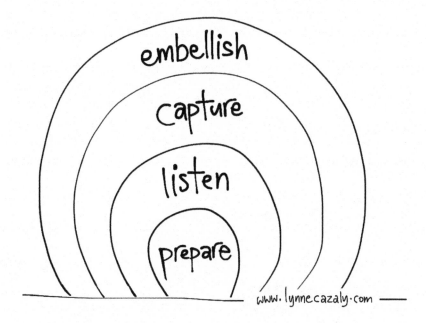

www.lynnecazaly.com

4. Embellish (time permitting)

When you have time, go back to your words, your scribbles or sketches, your images if you've sketched some, and your thinking and... pretty it up, embellish it.

When time permits. I'll do this often when working with teams and groups. I'll be capturing, facilitating, discussing, and working with the team. Then they'll be working on something as a team or in smaller groups. There's nothing for me to do but float about and check on progress or be available to guide or assist. So I'll go and embellish. I'll add extra words, some images and small icons or shapes, some colour, more detail, some shading, some more context, or put in some more information that extends the sense, that makes even more sense for people, quicker and clearer than before.

But there's a point. I think if you're spending way too long on the sketching part of making sense, you're getting a bit carried away. There's good enough and there's brilliant. And some of the overly brilliant art-y-ness of visual thinking and capture can be downright disheartening, threatening and super-status laden.

Who wants to add to a map that's looking all 'perfect'? I've had people say that they don't want to mark the chart, or 'ruin' the visual. So I'll go for a more low-fi approach. That way, it looks rough and hand crafted and imperfect and a rapid draft version. That invites contribution. It invites collaboration and it invites iteration. There is more that's possible. It says 'we're not finished yet. What could you add?'

This is a beautiful invitation to people.

Show what you mean
Henry Kissinger said: "the task of the leader is to get his people from where they are to where they have not been."

As a leader, you do what you've gotta do. I think a key role for contemporary leaders is that of the sense maker for the team or group. Not always in every meeting or setting, but in many.

So how are you intending to do this?

You know where you want them to go; you've got a mental image, a mind of possibilities and potential and a plan for how you'll bring that about. But you've got a tough time ahead, so many questions to answer, to help people get that picture into their minds.

The short cut to clarity is to show them what you mean.

We all recognise the Eiffel Tower, the Grand Canyon, the Pyramids - these 'things', objects and wonders of the world by their visual clarity.

So stop playing charades!

You've been trying to communicate using words, a thing that is most certainly a picture.

How much easier would Charades the game be if you could just show people a picture of the movie poster for 'Rear Window' rather than having to act it out : movie title, two words, first word, hmmmm, point to my rump, wait for responses and hilarity to ensue. Second word, draw out a square using your hands! Aha! See you're drawing and acting things out. You're drawing using your body - you're trying to create.... a PICTURE!

Stop talking, start showing.

Just show a picture - here, this is what I'm thinking about for this future vision. This is what I think the team could look like, the targets could be. How can we get there? What ideas do you have team?

Isn't this a distraction?
In my early days work with sensemaking and visual thinking I'd worked with some facilitators where I listen and sense make while they run a process with the group - think of consultation or decision making for example. Yet one facilitator didn't want to use a visual or sense making approach. She said it would be distracting and disconnecting. Rather, she finds it distracting.

Are the participants and team looking at the visual and not at her? She said that she feels they've disconnected from the conversation.

But this is the big problem. Too many workplace meetings are all talk. Too little thinking and way too little visualisation or concept mapping and sense making.

Of course people will shift their focus; they'll shift it to something more stimulating, interesting and engaging. Take the hint. The 'sit around the table and let's all talk' is boring as hell once you've done it a few times. It assumes that our preference is to sit. And listen. Louder voices are heard and those with great ideas and thinking just don't get the chance to put their thinking out there, drowned out by the higher volume players. Those who prefer to 'do' have no option but to 'sit and listen'. Why not make the visual the central element or the focus?

Let the conversation pivot around the visual. This is what we're talking about. Look at this. How can we shape, fix, modify, design, improve or eliminate this thing. Help people maintain focus. Give them something to more deeply connect to than heaps of talk. The map and the visual is actually a focusing tool, not a distracting tool.

The thinking not the drawing

When I'm running making sense, visual thinking, visual agility and visual facilitation programs, the 'I can't draw' complex is big. It's almost always spoken by someone in the room and if it's not spoken out loud in those words, it's felt. Deeply. Fearfully. There are dips of confidence and awkward moments of 'I'm not good enough' leaking out of many participants throughout the day.

But visual thinking and using it for making sense is not a drawing capability thing. Not a big capability anyway. Sure it can be a little capability. But it's more of a confidence thing.

People can be more uncertain about what they think rather than what they draw. Combine the two and you have people unsure that they'll be able to visually represent what they're thinking. I reckon that's the problem. 'Here's my thinking on that.' A list of dot points is tough to argue with. They're just points after all. But some well digested, thought over and packaged information - now that we can tear strips off!

So visual thinking is about the thinking, not the drawing. I think once you know about 20 or so icons, you're good to go. No need for practice to make perfect. Rough and hand crafted is just fine. Ask any craft beer connoisseur. It's the out of the ordinary, the different to everything else, the made by a human, the boutique nature of the craft that appeals. It's beer, but it's boutique.

They're visuals, but it's the thinking that makes them so, that makes them different, that makes the sense.

Let it breathe

You know when you're on a bus or train and it's crowded... the air conditioning isn't working. It's hot and steamy and packed. Not a nice way to travel. You can't wait to get off that moving tin can of sardines.

Same applies to capturing sense making content. Let it breathe. Give the words on that map you're making some white space. Or it gets hot and steamy, stinky and you just want to get way from it.

Order if important

I think we're obsessed with arrows and numbers. We're obsessed with the order of things or the order or sequence in which information was delivered. But I don't believe it's always important. Often it's just the end result that's really important. Or some of the steps along the way. But even then the sequence in which they were delivered or arrived at is not important.

Drop your arrows and numbers. Unless you absolutely need them to show that this came first, that was next and that thing was third, then go ahead, forget the numbers. You'll just confuse people, add more non-sense and add another layer of complexity and information that's superfluous and counter to the task at hand - which is making sense of it. I'll have some more to say on this later...

Organic if not

If the order isn't important, go for random and organic. Let things spring up on a page or white board wherever they do. It doesn't matter.

Start at the top. Or the bottom. Or the left or the right. Go crazy and start in the centre. I love that organic 'onion' and layers approach to building up of information on a sensemaking map. When the order doesn't matter and it's key points, arrange them in a ways that are random and non-sequential. Here, there, over there and this here.

Popcorn is hot

Picture this... a leader or team member approaches a whiteboard to make sense of a conversation happening in a meeting. They pick up a whiteboard marker - probably a dried out old pale green one or a red one that's all fluffy on the end with barely and ink left in it. They start to scrawl on the board. They start at the top of the page, write a #1, they write a key point. Underneath that they write #2, and then a key point... and on, down to oh... #7 or #11 or wherever the points get to.

I think bullet points are bullshit. I don't think they help with making sense. After a few points we've lost the point. Nothing is more important than the other, it's all so, so ... !

So play popcorn! Put the list into a random popcorn arrangement. When the first suggestion arrives, put it over on the right, the next one bottom left, the next top left, the next in the centre, the next somewhere else. Non-listy. Just organic and random.

Unless the order of this information matters, then put it wherever. I think a list indicates some priority or presumes connection. 'This came first, this came second'. Again, unless that is important in making sense of it, just get it on the page and don't worry where it's located.

Making Sense - Lynne Cazaly

Stories for Sense

In making senses, stories are critically important. Not so much the **telling** of stories, rather the **hearing**, the **distilling** and the getting to the **essence**. That's the sense part.

Even micro narratives, tiny little slithers of a story are worth grabbing and capturing. It could be a phrase, a statement, a couple of words, a slang term or a quote; when people drop these little micro gems into the conversation, look out, grab them and capture them. Reflect them. These will help you make sense.

It's a little like how panning for gold might give you hundreds or thousands of little pieces of golden glitter, but no big nuggets. Yet it's the mounting up of those little shimmers that can give you the right to say you've 'struck gold'.

So don't discount the little pieces of glitter, the little slithers of a story, the tiny segments or phrases or grabs. Together they can make some wonderful sense.

In sensemaking and making sense, you've got to tune in those listening skills to hear the slithers of stories; to listen to what people are saying and sharing with you… to capture those.

Don't just wait for facts and data. Engage in the anecdotes, the stories, the tales and the telling.

In my earlier career, my first career, I worked in public relations. Oooh, don't throw tomatoes or boo and hiss. It was good PR. It was community relations. I worked in public health, education, government, training, media, sport. It was about helping people understand what was going on and how they could either get involved … or run the other way!

Whatever the topic, project, program of work or PR piece I was working on, we always had to craft key messages. When you watch someone present to the media, and if they've been media trained, they'll be delivering their content in sound bites and key chunks - those repeatable, printable, quotable quotes that radio and television programs, like to broadcast. It's a short chunk of sweet loveliness on the topic.

Similarly I remember learning about 'actuality' when I did some work experience at the radio station FOX-FM in Melbourne, Australia. The news team was always keen to get some real human content that helped drive the message home and made sense of the whole news story.

The same happens in communication, leadership and workplaces everywhere. You need some sound bites and digestible chunks for the listeners and viewers to take in and understand.

Gather little slices, pieces, chunks and hints. Together they can give you incredible sense and help show what people are thinking, wondering, learning, sensing and making.

Map the stories you hear, capture them, visualize them, share them and reflect on them… put them together, for they will help you – and the people you're working with - make sense.

★ www.lynnecazaly.com

Mapping the Dialogue

Dialogue mapping is the activity of facilitating a conversation and capturing the threads. Once you've got some threads, you express them in a visual form – think words, plus images, shapes, symbols, arrows and lines.

If there are competing sides you might have an argument map or a pros and cons map.

The beauty of a dialogue map is that you don't let key content vapourise upward in the room back out through the air vents! No, you capture it and map it. It means others can see what is being said, in dialogue. It brings seemingly unrelated items together, creating a systems approach to thinking and conversations.

You can isolate questions.
And collate answers.

You can separate out the content of arguments, debates and rationale. You can highlight data, sources of information and research.

Connections and relationships, links and lines can be drawn. You start to see more than what you were just thinking. It's collected and shared, objectively.

I've found dialogue mapping to be one of THE most powerful tools working with groups. and different cultures, countries, fields, industries, levels of literacy, people with disabilities and in groups of large and small numbers.

'Hooray!' is what people often say when they see the product taking shape. They're finally able to see what's been sitting quietly in other people's heads!

Then once it's up there, further collaboration happens. Beyond the conversation, the chart, image and visual becomes an artifact of the conversation; it marks a time in history when sense was made based on what was known.

It helps people hear each other. Because we're not really listening are we. It helps capture complex content and represents the views of all, not just the loudest. It helps create shared understanding. Meetings are shorter, more gets done, it's a richer experience and it's highly engaging.

Further, Tom Wujec in his TEDU Talk *'Three ways the brain creates meaning'* reports on the 650 sketches that were created at an event with one of the founding fathers of visualization in the modern workplace, David Sibbet.

Wujec asks, what is it about illustrations and visuals that make meaning? He says that the brain doesn't actually see the world as it is, but it creates a bunch of 'a-ha' moments.

The Ventral stream part of the brain recognizes the 'what' something is, like when you give your brain a word. The Dorsal stream locates the object in physical body space, and creates a mental map in your mind. And then the Limbic system kicks in, deep in the brain and that's the part that feels; it's the gut centre.

So it's the combination of these that help us make meaning in different ways.

With visuals, Wujec adds, the eye is invited to dart around the page. A sort of 'visual interrogation' is going on. Above all, he suggests we use images to clarify our ideas.

Chunks and chapters of thinking

Chunk it up. Chunk it down. Whatever you do, chunk it. Chunk it real good!

There's too much information, depth, detail and complexity. Just break it down into chunks or chapters of thinking.

It's how we work with information like phone numbers or information we need to recall and remember. We break it down into a rhythmic sing-song style of delivery so we can remember it, transfer it, recall it and reuse it. No wonder we're lost when we lose our mobile phones and smart phones; all the data and phone numbers we need are in there. We don't have a need to chunk that data anymore.

But most of us could recall a phone number from our childhood homes.

575325. There's one. From my childhood.

Then they added in an 0 when the phone exchanges grew. 5705325.

Then they added a 9. 95705325.

Lots of little chunks. The 9570 then the 5325. The same goes for information.

Chunk it and chunk it real good. There's too much of it to expect people to stay interested, let alone remember anything. Yes, I've voiced my views on how bullet points are bullshit elsewhere. They're lazy. They're not chunked. They're not sense. They're non sense.

Mapping flow not order

Earlier I mentioned how I reckon we can all get a bit too obsessed with the order of things.

When I'm working with teams and groups or training people in visual sense making, I see so many people who believe (rightly or wrongly) they need to show the order of the information.

Don't get me wrong, sometimes that's right.

I don't believe that the order in which information was discussed or decided or talked about *always* needs to be visually mapped. The outcomes do and the key points do and the essence and main content do, for sure.

But the order in which it was delivered? Yeah, I don't think it's always as important or worth the worry, time and mental attention that we give it. Sometimes, yes. Always, no.

So if it's organic, just let it flow. Represent and capture and map it in any old order. The content matters, the sequence may not. May not.

But hey, when the order, number or sequence of something **is** important, then for sure, map it out and show it. Show where the thinking began, what came next, which bits came after that, which pieces were shifted, shaped or edited and which pieces were cut and thrown down onto the cutting room floor.

If sequence isn't important, stop worrying about it so much. Give your time and attention to listening better, mapping better, collaborating more and making sense.

Making Sense - Lynne Cazaly

What's on the horizon?

What's up there? Up ahead? Few people aren't interested in 'what's next'?

Ask any couple who's dating about when they might be moving in together... or getting engaged!

They get engaged and then everyone wants to know when they're getting married.

They get married and everyone wants to know when they're having a family.

They start a family and everyone wants to know when they're having another one.

They have another one and everyone wants to know if that's it or if there will be yet another one.

We're obsessed with 'what's next'.

Help people out by showing them what you *think* the horizon looks like. Granted you don't fully know what it *will* look like, but you must have some idea about a little further along the path.

And if you don't have any idea, then hint at what you think it might be like based on your best guess or your research or industry data or your hunches, views, thoughts, dreams or nightmares.

And if you don't know, ask. Ask others. That's big engagement right there!

Essence: not everything

It's sometimes hard to remember when you're knee deep listening to somebody waffle on in a meeting what this thing was all about.

Or when you're trying to take notes in a learning environment but you're inundated with content and sources and quotes and important dates and information.

Beware when you're mapping to make sense; you might be trying to capture everything. But don't. Stay cool ok?

Just work out what the big meaning or the heart of it is or the biggest of big pictures. Write that. Capture that. Map that.

Most of all, relax. Listen.

Pick up some threads.
Connect some dots.
Make some meaning.
Connect unrelated pieces.
See what comes out of that.

Get some key points and key chunks. down Don't worry so much about getting all of the 'everything'.

It's nothing. Really.

Just get some of the sense, the essence of it.

Present the sense you made

If you've been using a visual sense making and mapping approach and capturing content, mapping out thinking, planning out a possible vision, reflecting on the conversation, don't just stand there... present it.

Once the good work of sense making has been done, play it back. Rewind and present what you've heard, what you've captured and mapped and what it looks like.

This looping, review and presentation gives people the chance to hear and see it again. Further sense making occurs.

You might get to another level of depth and understanding.

This is a way better option than running out of the meeting room on the hour because another team has the room booked!

Allocate some time to appropriately wrap up the mapping part of sense making. In this way you close the loop for now on thinking and conversation and you show the progress you made and where you're at now.

What's missing?

I was capturing some content and sense making for an emergency management event. A room full of firefighters and emergency service personnel! Woo hoo!

But their important work was my focus, of course!

At the end of their conversation and meeting, I asked them: 'What's missing?'

Rather than packing up and getting the hell out of there, I stayed, lingered and let them process, review, talk further and, what I call 'marinate' the information.

I asked 'What's missing?'

They added some other points that didn't quite make it through the presentations from the leadership team. So we filled the gaps on charts, flip charts, posters and digital files. There were some specific phrases, words, sentences, concepts, programs, and acronyms. It was still important content and part of the mapping in the sense making process.

It gave them the opportunity to review what they'd been working on. It was a little like 'stopping the presses' before a magazine or newspaper is printed. What do you want to add, change, edit or alter?

Often we don't get this opportunity; or the reverse, we tinker and edit way too much and the document, information and content loses its sense and becomes a version of non-sense. It can become too vanilla and tasteless ad over tinkered.

Stay open to what else might be possible. Be open to what you might have missed in the mapping; what you may not have heard or what you may have interpreted or mapped in a way that wasn't intended.

Making Sense - Lynne Cazaly

21 Techniques for Making Sense

"The unknowable path might also be the right one.

The fact that your path is unknowable may be precisely *why* it's the right path.

The alternative, which is following the well-lit path, offers little in the way of magic.

If you choose to make art, you are no longer following. You are making.

- Seth Godin

Making Sense - Lynne Cazaly

21 Mapping Techniques for Making Sense

1. Compare the pair.
Show now vs then, how it was and how it is, the problem and what's needed, this option and that.

---

2. Plot a process.
Break it down. Simplify things.

---

3. Timeline.
Show the history. It's important to many people and helps validate what happened and how they feel about it. Let them have this. But it also shows growth, change, progress and evolution. Like the wall at home with names, ages and heights used to measure how tall the kids were growing.

4. Parts of the whole.

Zoom in to show how this part is part of the whole. Like the stops on a rail journey or the ingredients in a recipe or the individuals in a team.

---

5. Chunks 'n Categories.

Slice it up by chunking like with like or choosing a category. Just as Trivial Pursuit allows you to choose a category to fill your plastic pie of wedges, so too can sense makers. Help with sense making: chunk it up, categorise it down.

---

6. The Story of Everything.

When the scene or picture or vision is big big big, show the countries, cities, towns and villages. As you fly over a large expanse and break it down, the same for your vision. If you need to go bigger, go 'up' and 'out'. Think galaxy. Or universe!

Making Sense - Lynne Cazaly

7. Danger and Safety.

There's too much at risk to go non-sense with safety. Be a sensemaker, life saver and safety chaser. Beware of this, look out for that, step around that thing, use gloves when you touch this and make sure the safety guard is in place.

8. Instructions.

Safer working, simpler processes, clearer instructions. Imagine the airline safety card as one long sentence! All the elements of luggage, bracing, exits, oxygen are mapped out in visual instructional form. Same with workplace information. Map it out clearly, use visuals, short familiar words and chunks of content.

9. Metaphor.

So the title of the book goes *I never metaphor I didn't like...* so too goes it with humans and metaphors. They help us bootstrap or connect to something that we don't yet know. By understanding something familiar we can connect that to something as yet unfamiliar. While metaphors can be highly creative, they can be a little corny or twee. Take the classic, clichéd, iceberg. And while we're at it, I find the jigsaw puzzle a little overdone too. I think 'recipe' is getting into that territory too. Don't go corny; stay cool.

---

10. Report back or whip around.

Collate feedback, report backs or a collection of comments. By grouping a similar task or activity's information, you're making sense.

Making Sense - Lynne Cazaly

11. Who's on the Team?

A new team, new roles or changed responsibilities can be pretty tough to get your head around. So if you're leading the team - or on that team - get some sense about it. Map things out and show who's new, who's doing what, how it's different to before and what they're working on.

One team I worked with was creating their 'who's on the team' visual map and they took photos of each other and then drew little bodies with their hobbies and interests around them. Sounds a bit school class-ish? Actually it was highly engaging! It stimulated interest from other business units, got people asking questions and helped bring the team closer together for higher performance. Winners!

12. Please present a report.

It's totally cringe worthy when you're asked to present something and you dump all of that report information into a PowerPoint presentation. Boring. The best reports cover a range of different ways of making sense. Include snapshots, visuals, descriptions, graphs, and data - include a mix. Map it out, make sense for people. Why not bring the power of an infographic to work in your report?

13. The product showcase.

Customers, clients and buyers just don't know your product range as well as you do. There's the hint. Get to sense making as soon as you possibly can. Bring them in to the conversation, presentation and collaboration. Make sense of the product, what it does, how it does it and most of all, why you have it in your product showcase.

14. Then. Now. Next.

This is one of the most fundamental ways of sense making. It's telling the past, present, future story. It helps validate people who have been involved in the past, it welcomes people to the work that's being done now and it paints a picture and makes sense about what will be happening in the future.

---

15. Welcome.

The first day at a new school can make you feel lost. Same happens in workplaces. Where are the bathrooms, where are the best cafes, where is the local station or bus stop, where is the best place to park? All of these 'this is how you might like to do things around here' stuff can help new members of the team get to grips and get to sense making as soon as possible.

---

16. We do it like this.

Policies, procedures, processes and any type of step-by-step or values and behaviour thing in your organisation, unit, team or workplace needs to be made sense of swiftly. It takes too long to just pick it up through osmosis. Make sense quickly. Tell visual stories and bring a range of different modes to bear on information that's often presented in detailed, dull, drawn-out waffle.

17. Data or Details.

Share your data, numbers and details with a symbol, image or icon. Keep it segregated. Make it interesting... worth the effort of looking at and reading it.

18. It's connected like this.

When you need to show connections, relationships, networks and associations of any sort, get to sense making. If you think just a couple of words with some arrows between them will do the trick, you need to think again. Make more sense of it. Beyond a direct arrow, there's likely more going on here. It's more than an arrow or line. Take time, make sense, show how. Metaphors can work; think maps, trees, paths, journeys, rivers, creeks, mountains, paths, spokes on a wheel - these all show how things can be connected.

19. It's because of this.

Cause and effect relationships are pretty common. We often need to show that 'this' happened which caused 'this' and then 'this'. The flow, connection and relationship can be made clear. Clearer than a list of points on a page or a paragraph of twaddle.

20. Storytelling.

The rise of storytelling in organisations and business can't be denied. Books are blossoming and leaders are getting authentic by sharing snippets from their life in an effort to engage and inspire. The moral of the story is make meaning and share meaning. It's a perfect step to sense making. The end.

21. The Manifesto.

Unwritten ground rules and manifestos can be strong documents and visual tools to capture and represent key content. Manifestos spring from the Italian word *manifestare*, originally Latin and meaning to make public or make obvious. It's about going public with your information, especially before change.

32 Templates for Making Sense

"Breakthrough insights aren't manufactured like widgets in a factory. They dawn on us in nascent form, like the sight of a vague shape on the horizon. They are first present in our mind and bodies in a preverbal state, an inkling, a feeling. Some refer to this as the "slow hunch.""

From 'The Moment of Clarity: Using the Human Sciences to Solve Your Toughest Business Problems'

- Christian Madsbjerg, Mikkel B. Rasmussen

ABoVe the LINE
BeLOW the LINE

www.lynnecazaly.com

1. Above the Line/Below the Line

What's acceptable and what's not? What's believable and what's not? What will you include, what will you exclude?

The above the line/below the line map helps you separate content, ideas, information and thoughts.

Use the line to divide your map and sort or categorise thinking.

Line

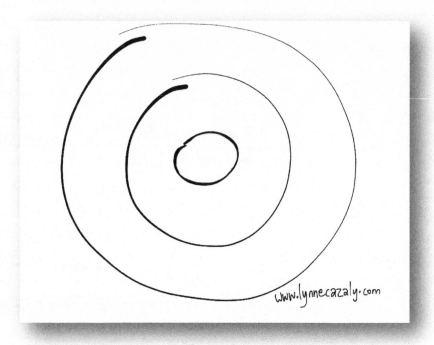

www.lynnecazaly.com

2. Target or Bullseye

Start in the centre and then move out; or start out there and move closer to the centre. Dart boards, targets, goals and circles. You could label the circles or put multiple labels among

Target

Making Sense - Lynne Cazaly

www.lynnecazaly.com

3. Clusters and Clouds

Some thoughts may be still in the making... not yet formed... all 'cloud-like' and fluffy. Capture them in thought bubbles or cluster them in like groups. Connect them or keep them separate.

Clouds

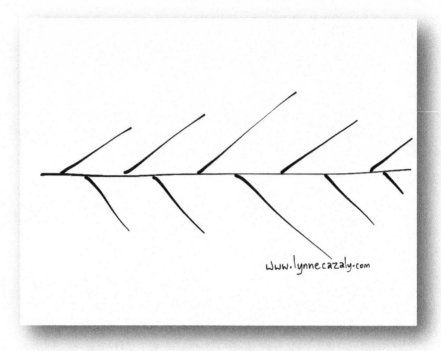

www.lynnecazaly.com

4. Fishbones, Branches and Arms

Is there a main chunk or path? What comes off that?
Are there smaller and lighter branches that spear outwards from there?
Is there fruit on the branch? Leaves or foliage?
Is there a critical path that needs to be followed before other things can be done?
What is the main spine or bone of the thinking? Are there knowns and unknowns along that main branch?
Think also of pipelines and wiring and tunnels and other connected and branched metaphors.

Branches

www.lynnecazaly.com

5. Tables and Columns

Lists and columns are sooooo overused, overdone and overrated. They're lazy and easy and yes, they're logical and linear… but they're less engaging, inspiring, communicative and creative than many of the other visual maps at your disposal.

OK, settle down, don't delete them all together. While I'm not a huge fan of tables and columns, go ahead and use them when that's what your thinking, mapping and making of sense is about: lists, columns, rows and categories.

But go through and look at the other 39 maps and templates here before you go and get a severe case of column-tableitis.

Tables

6. Funnels, Filters and Sieves

What needs to be filtered out?
What are you starting with and what will the process be along the way?
What ingredients will you start with...what happens to them...are there a number of filters ?
What does each filter do?
What is the end product?
What will drop out of the bottom?

Filter

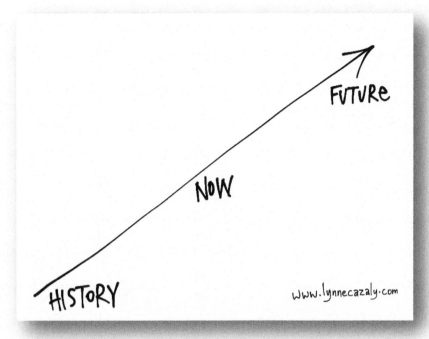

7. A Line to the Future

Timelines that run from then to now and project towards the future. The history was then, this is now, what might be next? Show the thinking in a straight line, mapping out a path or a trajectory. Connect the past with the present and linked to the future.

Future Line

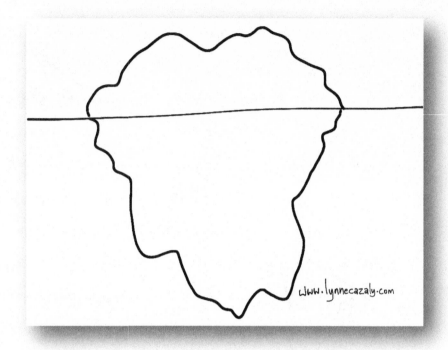

www.lynnecazaly.com

8. Icebergs

Icebergs are a little clichéd… but anyway… if you must…

What's visible, above the surface?
What can you see from a distance?
What's easily observable?
What lies beneath?
What can't we see – what are we underestimating?
What else is there that's connected to the stuff we can see?
What might we be missing?
What don't people know about… yet?

Iceberg (yawn)

9. Scope/Focus

Looking through a telescope or binoculars you have the
opportunity to point them in a direction, to focus them in and
keep some things 'in' focus and others out of the picture.
Where are you looking?
What's in focus, what's in scope?
What will be out of the picture?
What are you still not sure of – what's up for debate and
discussion?

Scope

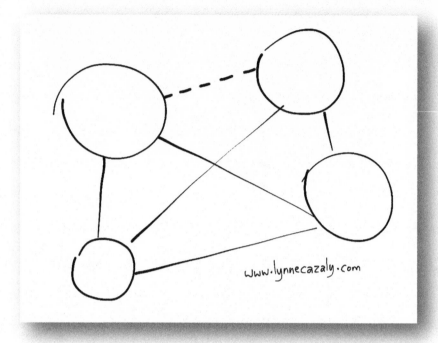

10. Networked and Connected

Are there individual things and elements, but they also have a connection and relationship to other things? Show me. Show them. Get it out there and make it visible so it can be worked on, talked about, managed, created, developed.

Which pieces are connected to which?
Do they have strong, solid connections or dotted lines?
Do larger circles convey something?
What does it mean?

Network

www.lynnecazaly.com

11. Ladder

Take it to a metaphor with a ladder, another version of the triangle, the evolution, with steps, stages and progress.

Label the levels, indicate where you're at and what's next. What's way up there, in the clouds, not reachable ... yet?

Ladder

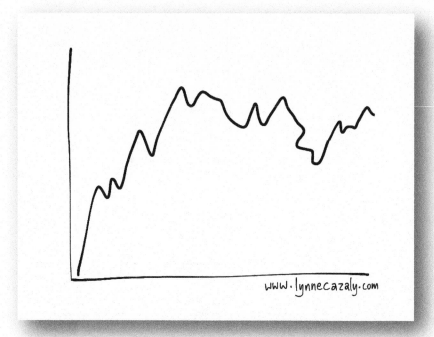

12. Graphs and Charts

Going up, going down, up and down: plot it and connect the dots… that's what connecting the dots is about. Show people what it looks like so they know. Trend is your friend.

Data and information will only convey so much − show people what it looks like so they can get that swift snapshot of where things have been and where they're heading.

Graph

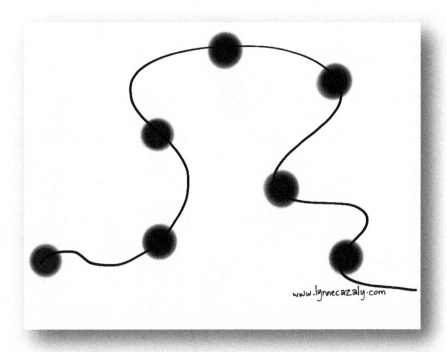

www.lynnecazaly.com

13. Paths and Journeys (up)

Starting lower left and following a mainly Western view of going to the right. Map out a path of waypoints or signs, stops or places.

Where is this thing going?
How will you show what comes next?
Is there a hill or peak, a climax or ultimate place to reach?
Is it all downhill from there…?

Path

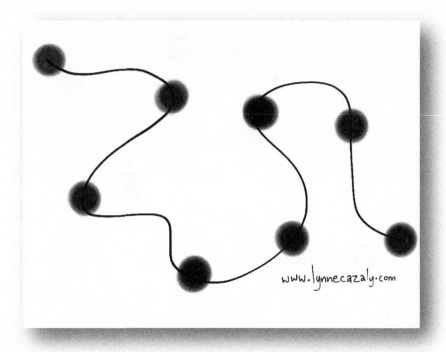

www.lynnecazaly.com

14. Paths and Journeys (down)

Starting at the top left, there are ups and downs, a longer path
or journey.
What are the stops along the way?
Where does the winding path go?

Another Path

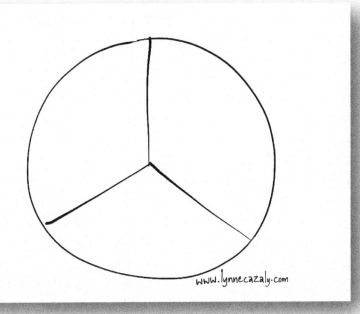

15. Pies and Graphs

Go beyond just a number. Show me how much it is compared to other things. Show me a pizza or pie slice, a segment or a lemon or lime or other fruit sliced up. Cheesecake anyone?

Statistics and numbers are more easily understood with a visual snapshot.

Pie

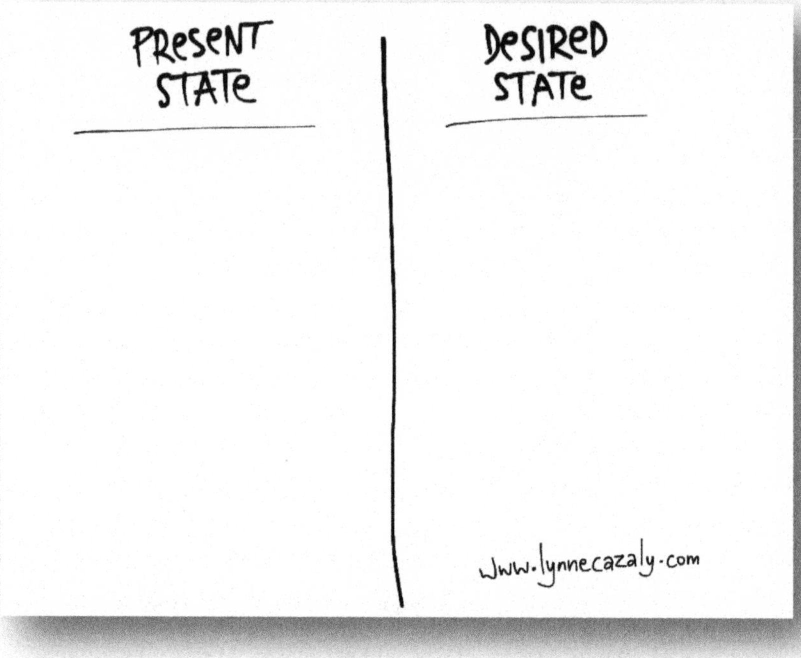

PRESENT STATE | DESIRED STATE

www.lynnecazaly.com

16. Present State – Future State/This & That

How are things now?
What's the current reality?
Where do you want to get to?
How do things need to change?
What does the future look like?

This/That

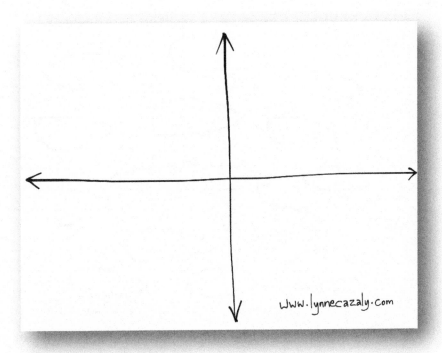

www.lynnecazaly.com

17. Quadrants & Squares

The consulting world is built on them!
Get two continuums, cross them.
Which ones work well upward, downward, sideways?
Which quadrant is preferred, which is less so … or perhaps
they are all important.
Number them - which one is first?
Then which one next?

Square

www.lynnecazaly.com

18. Clumps and Chunks, Organic and Random

Just let it flow and randomly drop information, ideas and content on a page wherever it lands.

Let process, order and numbering go for now.

Maybe the ideas un-connected will help people find connections and links that you weren't thinking of.

Onion skins, layers upon layers, hidden depths and what's at the heart.

Random, organic, layers.

Organic

Making Sense - Lynne Cazaly

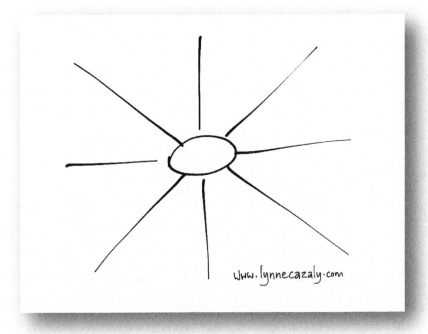

www.lynnecazaly.com

19. Spokes

Start in the centre, at a hub. Then radiate out.
What are the little islands of information that your spokes or thoughts can connect to?

What is at the heart or the centre?

Are there satellite sites around the outside… with other spokes creating new hubs?

Spokes

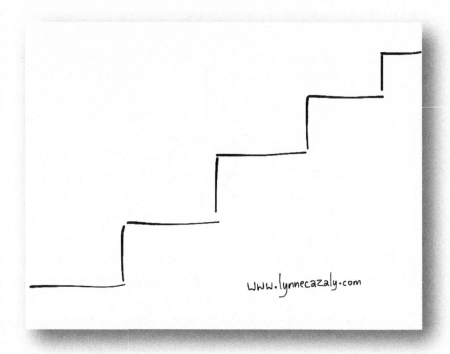

20. Steps... Step it Up

Lifting up, stepping up or moving up. Show it visually.
What's the first level or step?
What's next?
What will it take to get to that next level?
How will we lift?

Steps

Making Sense - Lynne Cazaly

www.lynnecazaly.com

21. Storyboards

The advertising industry knows the secret of communicating segments of information. Scenes, snapshots and storyboards show a slice of life. A snippet or segment.

Show a bigger or longer story by capturing only the critical points.

Chunk it up, chunk it down, put it in a box and make a cell. Think cartoonist or filmmaker or creative storyteller: how would they show this?
How would they explain it, communicate it and make sense of it?

Storyboard

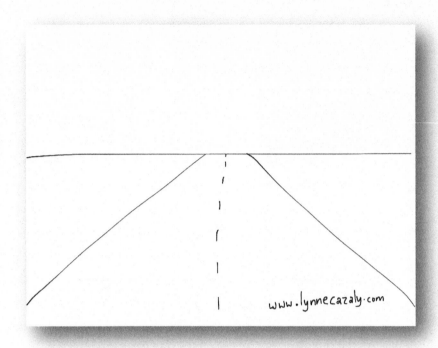

www.lynnecazaly.com

22. Roads and Horizons

What's nearest us… where we are now?
What's next?
What's way up there?
What can't we see yet?
What's on the horizon?
How will we get there?
Who's driving?
Do we have snacks?

Road

23. Then, Now and Next - Columns

Another version of the past, present and future. That was then, this is now, here's what's next. Map it out – in columns this time. Now we can see the progress or path and how things will be different.

Columns

24. Trees

It's all about growth; roots, a trunk, clusters of foliage (that look a lot like thought bubbles – maybe we haven't defined them just yet... maybe they're still growing?)

What seeds are we planting that will come to fruition?
What roots us to the ground? What can't we change?
What is a sturdy, strong trunk?
What are the branches or elements that we're working on growing?

Making Sense - Lynne Cazaly

www.lynnecazaly.com

25. Triangles and Hierarchies

Is it built on a foundation?
Do this, then do that, before you do that?
Throw it in a triangular model with levels stepping up.
Perhaps it's 3D with sides to that triangle.
Maybe it's inverted.
Where are things pointing?
Where is the base – where is the top?

Triangles

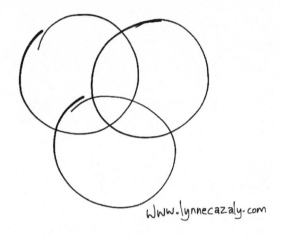

www.lynnecazaly.com

26. Venn it

Three things - or two - that interact and impact each other.
Move on from bullet points – because bullet points are bullshit.
Show me more than a freakin' list.
How do these interact, connect, relate… or not?
Are they intersecting – or are they separate, apart?

Venn

www.lynnecazaly.com

27. Journey, Road or Path –Winding Road

The journey of change, the road map, the path to possibility.

What do they look like?
Where might we stop on the way?
Will there be any barriers or hurdles?
How do we know when we're there?
Few paths are straight – there are always surprises, hurdles and potholes along the way!

Winding Road

28. Signposts, Stops and Markers

Along this path we may pass many signs, stops or markers.
What are they?
Why are they there?
Why do we need to take note of them?
Do we have to stop… slow down or just read them?
What do they mean?
How do they relate to the bigger picture?
What are the messages they convey?

Signs

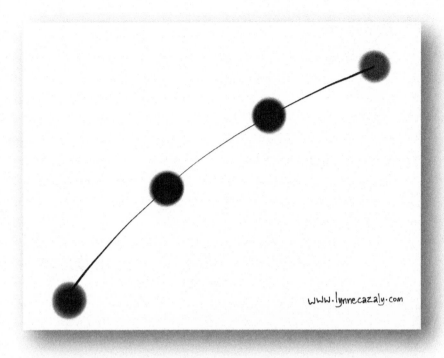

www.lynnecazaly.com

29. Arc, Sweep or Stretch

Overarching, far-reaching, stretching and spanning.
Perhaps what we're thinking about stretches over a distance, time or space.
Show how expansive it is, what's first, what's next and where it is going.

Like the planets in our solar system or a future trip to Mars, an arc, sweep or stretch shows there is distance, time and light into the future.

Arc

30. Continuum

Is there here…. and there?
Then map them out on a line.
Is it all this and all that… and the option of something in the
middle? Show us.
What's the scale, the spectrum, the breadth and the range?
Is it all or nothing, black or white or a bit of grey?
Where are we on the scale?

Like a tightrope walker balancing on a high wire, wavering one
way and then the other … and then holding steady.

Continuum

www.lynnecazaly.com

31. Timeline

Showing and acknowledging where you've been is a powerful validation tool. It helps acknowledge the past, acknowledge the challenges or the path to get to here. With a timeline you'll get a picture of progress over time, whether it is hours (think of how the media uses a timeline to show the steps leading up to a critical situation) or days, weeks, months or years.

During a year-long leadership program, the team timelined their year at their final retreat. It was a reflection, a gathering of content and a pulling together of an action-packed year. Missed moments were recollected, hidden gems were revealed and the depth of content covered over the course of the year was truly put on show. People got the full picture of a year they may have otherwise struggled to take in. It gave them a wide view, a timeline view.

Timeline

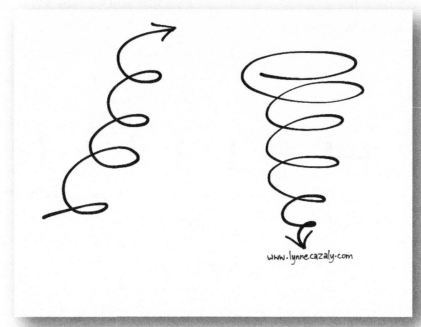

www.lynnecazaly.com

32. Spirals of Iteration

Show the twister in it - where is it going?
Is it moving up or down?
Sideways perhaps?
Big spirals or little, spinning in infinity or finding an end?
Where is the movement – fast or slow?

Spirals

Making Sense - Lynne Cazaly

ACT

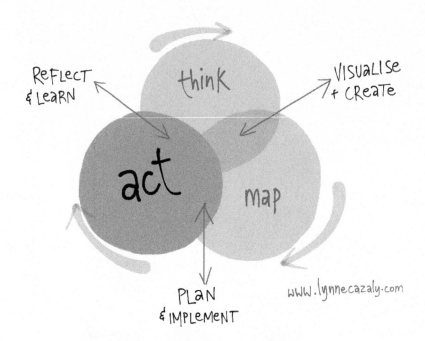

REFLECT & LEARN

think

VISUALISE + CREATE

act

map

PLAN & IMPLEMENT

www.lynnecazaly.com

Experiment. Try. Do

This third stage of making sense is where action is the imperative.

You've thought, you've mapped, now it's time to do. To act.

Too often, we think and talk and partially map and then back away from action. We break the momentum and stall. We don't do. In fact... we don't! Whether fear, indecision, red tape or plenty more of VUCA is contributing to the situation, something stops us as individuals, teams and organisations from putting our thinking and mapping in to practice, bold action and practice.

Yet it's through experimenting, trying, testing it out (and failing) that we get stuff done. We learn, reflect, adjust and adapt. We've done it all our lives. Why do we get so hesitant at work?

When we try and fail and learn and reflect, we go again and think some more, map some more and put more of our work into practice.

It's then that we are able to make sense; it's the retrospect, the hindsight that helps us truly make sense.

Don't delay, dilly-dally or dick around. Go and do.

Will we, won't we, maybe, ummm

Indecision is such a business and momentum killer.

Think of a meeting or conversation; there are ideas, possibilities, but then it all screeches to a halt because there isn't a decision.

Or wait, here's the decision: lets set another meeting date and talk about it all again next time. Urgh!

I think we are losing the drive to decide. And with that, the potential and power of sensemaking gets lost.

Yet decisions are such a vital component of leadership. They help you choose a course of action. They set a direction. They help express your leadership. They give people some certainty in this crazy uncertain world.

How about this: earlier this week I heard of more than 30 team members being on the receiving end and consequences of the indecision of a senior manager in a large organisation ... the leader couldn't decide what to do with the most important part of their strategy day, which is just a few days away.

What? It's a big and important strategy day. And it's that big and important and you can't decide!? You still have no certainty on what you want to achieve, how you will do that, and you're still oscillating and circulating and debating and ruminating over what could possibly be done.

And it's a strategy day. And it's important. And it's involving other people. And it's about the future of the team and what you work on.

Making Sense - Lynne Cazaly

Whatever the details and the whys and wherefores and 'yeah but maybe theys' that you may be scripting in your mind about this situation, the point here is that a decision wasn't made.

Over a period of time. No decision.

There's a lack of leadership right there. It's non-sense.

It's indecision, oscillation and hesitation and it doesn't help momentum or give a team strong leadership in uncertain environments.

Contemporary leaders **must** give their teams some certainty over the stuff they CAN give certainty on. And making decisions is one of them. Decisions help give people certainty.

Leadership is about making heaps of decisions. Every day.

Deciding which things you will tell, which you'll share, ask or do; which things will you:
- **Instigate**
- **Delegate**
- **Escalate**
- **Mitigate.**

It's that flipping from one view to another, unable to make a call or to put a marker in the sand... it's that 'dicking around' I call it, the not deciding that is a momentum and engagement killer.

Do we fear that:
- it will be the wrong decision
- it could really stuff things up
- maybe it's not totally right
- is it the best we can possibly do, maybe we can do better later with a bit more time
- stuffing this up will hurt my career
- maybe this will cause conflict

... and a bunch of other hesitation hang-ups.

Along with authenticity, clear communication and setting visions, leaders dear leaders, you need to make a FREAKING DECISION. And make it fast. Make one now. And make it a decision of action. That is what making sense is ultimately about: action that you can make sense of.

Failing Fast

If it doesn't work, that is also known as 'failing fast'. And you will soon know if it's not right. Failure and failing fast is very 'now'; it's contemporary, hip and the done thing in agile teams and organisations. But you've got to decide so you can act and then see what happens. If you don't decide, then you're not leading.

If you're not making a decision you're not stepping into action, you're not running an experiment and you're not leading. You're lying... in waiting.

Dangerously Safe

It's like you are balancing on a high wire, not moving towards the end goal and neither are you reversing or backing up to go along some other high wire. You don't even have anything to help you balance on that wire. You're a balance-less high wire walker. And that's dangerous.

You're putting yourself in a situation where a little gust of wind, a little rattle on the high wire is something that could topple you over. That wouldn't be a good ending.

An End to Choice

To decide. It means to end and terminate the choices you have. It means to 'cut off'. Don't be the person or role that someone else decides to cut off because you're not making decisions in your team or organisation. Decisions are leadership. Action is making sense. Do it. Make decisions, act, lead.

Pick up speed

I think you can go faster; go faster from thinking of something, to mapping it out and then to bringing it to fruition, to reality. In my view, there's too much talking, not enough action.

If you're concerned that everyone hasn't had their say yet or you haven't consulted enough yet or perhaps they may not agree with what you're proposing, just put it forward. I think more rapid thinking and rapid prototyping would save us all a lot of time, energy, waste and pain.

Get your initial thoughts together, get them into a form so they can be shared, create the first version or prototype of it and start testing that out. This could be a simple sketch; it could be a handmade version using Lego, or using and improvising with objects and tools around you.

It could mean crafting something up out of cardboard or paper.

Just freakin' do it - in that way, you'll see what you're thinking, and most importantly, so will others.

Retrospectives and looking back

Some well-regarded psychological advice for happiness is to avoid dwelling on your thoughts or living in the past; in the words of Dr Richard Carlson, it's best to *Stop Thinking, Start Living.*

But in a business and commercial sense, it can indeed be helpful to look back so we can make sense of what's been going on.

Sensemaking

That's how us humans make sense of things and connect the dots; we look back. Hindsight; it is 20-20 vision after all!

As little events occur through life, we often don't make connections between them as they're occurring, but when you look back, you can see with hindsight that there is sense to be made. A BIG sense. It's known as 'sensemaking'.

You'll often hear people exclaim '*I KNEW that was gonna happen*' or '*you could SEE what was going on from the get go*'.

We pick up clues and cues and our minds do the figuring out and the connecting of facts and happenings to make a plausible, possible explanation.

In a world of constant change, being able to make sense quicker becomes a strong competitive advantage.

Back to the Future

With a Back to the Future day happening in late 2015 it's a sweet reminder of past, present and future. This is when Marty McFly and Dr Emmet Brown in the film *Back to Future Part II* went back in time and then forward to the future (which occurred in real time on October 21, 2015). We can apply a similar way of thinking in our own lives and businesses... even if we don't quite have the time machine... yet.

Make Sense
So yes, go back in time; look at what happened, and make sense of it.

In a while you'll be able to make progress, then look back, make sense and learn again.

In agile software development, it's known and adopted frequently as the Retrospective. This is where the team discusses what was successful, what could be improved and how to incorporate that into the future. In planning and strategy circles, an approach called backcasting is used.

Make Decisions
Then you can go forward and because you know what you know, you can make decisions about the best steps forward for you and the team.

Make Progress
While it's easy, fun and distracting to look at bright shiny objects, cat videos and dogs in swimming pools, unless you're learning and reflecting on what happened, you won't make sense and you won't make progress.

You'll get a sad case of FOMO. You'll miss out on picking up trends, joining dots and making sense... and you won't be prepared for the **VUCA** (volatility, uncertainty, complexity, ambiguity) of now and the crazy future that continues to roll out up ahead.

Set your time machine mind to make sense regularly, so you can reflect, learn and get ready for the future.

So what could stuff this up?

A few things can get in the way of good, effective sensemaking.

Deborah Ancona suggests that because we need sensemaking when things are tough - think a crisis or challenge or minor freaking out - it's this exact state of mind that stops us being particularly good at making sense.

That's where the collaboration part can help. You know how you can have a good friend 'talk you down' if you're up in chaos and anxiety. They help you calm down.

Another thing that can stop smoother sense making progress is a dependence on direction. We're being a bit of a child, waiting for our parent (leader) to tell us what to do or to guide us. It's connected to fear, fear of doing the wrong thing, fear of getting in to trouble and being put in the naughty corner - or placed on performance management!

Even in the most challenging crises and complex situations, I find when facilitating making sense sessions, just let people be and treat them like humans, adult humans, all grown up and experienced and knowledgeable.

Sure we can have a little tantrum over the uncertainty and unknown but if you don't judge it, let it be, acknowledge and validate it 'yes this is a tough question, or tricky environment or challenging situation', then all will be well.

There was a time I was about to facilitate a three day strategic offsite for a private company. Big bucks to get everyone there. Lots of great decisions to make.

At morning tea, something didn't feel right. Intuition kicks in. I ask the Chairman and owner at the break – 'How are you going? Is everything ok?'

'No it's not. We're in financial shit', he says. 'Oh,' I say. 'Well maybe we should work on that after the break!'

We both laughed and then we got into it after the break. He was deeply embarrassed, ashamed, felt guilty, but we just got on with it and made sense of the information we had and decided what we would do.

By afternoon tea break, a couple of hours later, we were back on track and rocking a new strategy.

The company has since grown its greenfield development sites, acquired other businesses and is going great. I'll never forget the vulnerability, the fear he had of being the Chair and having that information in him.

So you may ask many questions - why didn't others know, why hadn't they worked that out earlier, why did they wait until financial shit before doing something? They're great sensemaking questions. Great questions. Hold on to them for when you need to do some making of sense next!

Let's learn this

Making sense is a capability and it's a learning program I've developed and delivered over recent years.

Many people experience it in the guise of visual thinking, critical thinking, insight gathering or visual facilitation.

It's not about the drawing. It's about your thinking, connections, visualising stuff, communicating that and being able to act on it and iterate it where needed.

Many of use spend a lot of time working in complex environments such as projects, technology and industries that are undergoing massive change, disruption and transformation.

One industry that's ripe for the use of sensemaking is software and technology. Many already use agile methods and frameworks that are about being responsive, adaptive and changing, so it's such a good fit.

So yes, leaders need this capability as the future of work shows us.

You can learn it by doing; that's the best way. You can work with others. Self assess. Keep a journal. Play the 'what would I do' game when you see a challenge or situation in another industry.

In hindsight it's so much easier.
In hindsight it makes so much more sense.

That's why you've got to explore stuff, think about it and talk about it, map it and then act.

Then you'll be able to explore more, map some more, act some more and keep it spinning.

Making Sense - Lynne Cazaly

40 Thought Starters for Making Sense

"If everyone waited to become an expert before starting, no one would become an expert. To become an expert, you must have experience. To get experience, you must experiment! Stop waiting. Start stuff."

Richie Norton

Author
The Power of Starting Something Stupid
and
Résumés Are Dead and What to Do About It.

Distill

Get to the point.
Help people understand
you swiftly by distilling
your thinking, *before* you
start speaking.

{1.}

Elastic

Remain flexible, willing to be stretched in your thinking, speaking and working.
Where are you being rigid?
What could you let go of... or at least loosen your grip?

{2.}

Focus

Give a clear indication of what the emphasis and focus is.
Which pieces are more important than others?
Out of everything, what should people pay attention to?

{3.}

Force

Use constraints to force or draw conclusions, to get to an end point or to bring about an outcome … especially when there is delay or hesitation. Just get one outcome or conclusion and you can keep momentum to reach for more.

{4.}

Central

Identify a starting point.
What is central or what
is a main hub of
thought?
What do things pivot
around?
What radiates out from
that hub?

{5.}

Piece

Indicate when information is a piece of something else.
Which piece is it?
Where does it fit?
What else does it connect to?
Are all the pieces there… or is something missing?

{6.}

Essence

Find and explain the key quality of it. What is so intrinsic and essential to it that it would not 'be' without it?

{7.}

Shape

Bring it in to form.
What shape is this idea,
information or thing?
What does it look like?
How would you
describe it?

{8.}

Making Sense - Lynne Cazaly

Radiate

Is this thing moving? Where could it go? Where does it need to go? Who needs to see it? How can it be shared?

{9.}

Angle

Look at things from a different position, point and perspective.
How does it change?
What else is possible?
What impact does your location have on how things seem, look, are?

{10.}

Pivot

Turn, move and shift.
Pivot when you least expect to.
Use the pivot as a creative tool to find yourself somewhere else.
Look somewhere else.
Look over there!
Move.

{11.}

Point

What is the main point?
If you had to bring it all down to this, just this one thing… what would it be?
Is there a single word, a short phrase or a sentence that this is about?

{12.}

Making Sense - Lynne Cazaly

Style

How many ways can you share or shape this information?

Think of eras of history and how they are recognisable by the style of the time.

What makes this the way it is?

What is the fashion of this?

{13.}

View

What does it look like from where you are right now?

Are you close or far away?

What about the view that others have?

What does it look like from their position or view?

{14.}

Drawn

Make a quick sketch it.
Any part of it.
Any shape of it.
Bring pieces together
visually or verbally
through your speaking,
writing, pointing and
linking.

{15.}

Together

A relationship can exist between two seemingly opposite pieces. Anything can be linked to anything. But which pieces belong together... and which absolutely don't?

{16.}

Distinct

Something may stand out above all else.
It stands taller, louder, broader or it's just more important.
What stands apart from the rest?

{17.}

Converge

Bring some things
together.
Where do they meet?
Do they cross over?
Do they diverge again?
Connect some related
pieces.

{18.}

Appreciate

Accept that there are other ways of seeing, thinking, learning and wondering.
What does that make you think?
Shift position; what would you not normally think?
See that possibility.

{19.}

Couple

Pair up.
For now or for ever.
Bring like pieces
together. Or bring
different together.
Watch what happens.

{20.}

Listen

What is said?
How is it said?
What is said first,
second, third?
What is said last?
What does it sound like?
What is not being said?

{21.}

Craft

Make, deliver and share. The human ability to make something brings a special quality. Hand made, human and helpful. What could you make and then share… to help make sense?

{22.}

Least

What doesn't belong?
Or needs to be at the
bottom of the list?
It's there … but it's not
in the spotlight.

{23.}

Link

Connect two or more. Are they similar or different? Are they close or far apart? How are they connected? What's so special, unique or relative about them?

{24.}

Linear

Start here and keep
going, straight.
Don't stop.
Stay on track, stay true
to the line.
Map it out in a
sequence.
Line it up.

{25.}

Last

How do you know
you're at the end?
Where is the finish line?
What makes it
THE END?
Celebrate getting there
and identifying
what it is.
You are done.

{26.}

Story and Narrative

Share the story about this.
Who is in it?
How did it start?
What happened?
How did it end up?
Share.
Repeat.

{27.}

First

What's most important, top of mind and the beginning?
But beware: just because it is mentioned first, may not mean it is intrinsic, critical or cornerstone.

{28.}

Modeling

Create it before you make it.

What does it look like?

What is the form, shape, style and structure?

Sketch it or prototype it.

Make it from dough, paper, cardboard, Lego or toys.

3D printer anyone?

{29.}

Replay

Listen to yourself again - what are you saying and thinking?
Listen to them… those humans. Listen again. Hear it. Record it and replay it. Write what they said. Rewind and press pause. What was it really about? What are they not saying? What else do you need to ask?
{30.}

Making Sense - Lynne Cazaly

Task

Break it down.
A piece here, a chunk there. Smaller bites can make bigger things happen. Focus on a single step or task that is digestible, achievable, applaudable.... appendable.

{31.}

Sense

What do you feel about this? What is it about? What is your gut telling you? What do you reckon will happen? Trust that you have a sense about this.

{32.}

Making Sense - Lynne Cazaly

Transparency

Show it and share it. Clarity comes from seeing. Put it out there. What was hidden that needs to be revealed, explained, shown or uncovered?

{33.}

Theme

What is the word, the colour, the era, the type, the toy, the song, the movie, the fashion, the thing? How can you tie it all together? What umbrella does it sit under?

{34.}

Message

A few words… a capsule of content that is easily shared.
What is the take away, the message from all of this?
What do you really want people to *know*, *think* or *do* about this?
What do people need to hear?
What is at the heart?

{35.}

Context

Go bigger picture. What does it look like from up there?

Where is it going?
How does it look from 20000 feet?

Go higher, go bigger. What is that about?
What does it look like from space?

{36.}

Making Sense - Lynne Cazaly

Meaning

How might this apply to others? What is it about for those affected or impacted? What about those who don't know anything about this - how might they see it? What meaning and bias are you putting on this? How can you shape it for another group, audience or target?

{37.}

Relate

How do pieces connect and impact each other? If they are not geographically together, how do they influence each other? What is similar, same or matching? What is different?

{38.}

Reverse

Work backwards. It's called 'breakthrough thinking' or backcasting. Go to the end where you've made sense. Work backward…what happened before that, and before that, and then before that. Bring the future forward.

{39.}

Déjà vu

Have you seen this before?

What was it like that time?

Is it similar but a little different?

Or is it different but the same?

What can you imagine happening this time?

{40.}

Making Sense - Lynne Cazaly

MAKING SENSE

A Handbook for the Future of Work

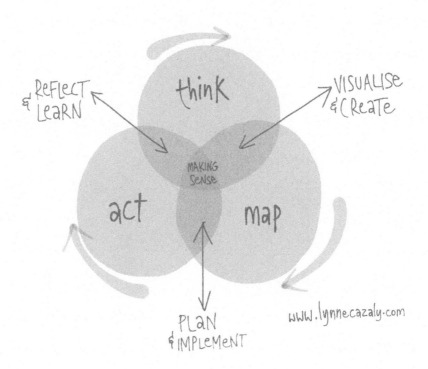

think

REFLECT & LEARN

VISUALISE & CREATE

MAKING SENSE

act

map

PLAN & IMPLEMENT

www.lynnecazaly.com

⭐ www.lynnecazaly.com

REFERENCES & READING

Achi, Zafer, and Jennifer Garvey Berger. "Delighting in the Possible." *McKinsey Quarterly*. McKinsey & Company, Mar. 2015. Web. 20 May 2015.

Ancona, Deborah. "Sensemaking: Framing and Acting in the Unknown." The Handbook for Teaching Leadership: Knowing, Doing, and Being. By Scott A. Snook, Nitin Nohria, and Rakesh Khurana. Thousand Oaks: SAGE Publications, 2012. 3-19.

Ancona, Deborah, Thomas Malone, Wanda Orlikowski, and Peter Senge. "In Praise Of The Incomplete Leader." *IEEE Engineering Management Review*: 29-37.

Baer, Drake. "Here's Why Companies Are Desperate to Hire Anthropologists." *Business Insider*. March 31, 2014

Bhargava, Rohit. *Non-Obvious: How to Think Different, Curate Ideas & Predict The Future*. N.p.: Ideapress, 2015. Electronic.

Bernstein, Elizabeth. "It's Healthy to Put a Good Spin on Your Life." *WSJ*. Dow Jones & Company, 6 Apr. 2015. Web. 20 May 2015.

Borrás, Susana, and Leonard Seabrooke, eds. *Sources of National Institutional Competitiveness: Sense-making in Institutional Change*. New York: Oxford UP, 2015.

Brittany. "Bilingual People's Brains Work In A Different, More Effective Way." *TruthTheory*. N.p., 19 Jan. 2015. Web. 20 May 2015.

Brougham, Greg. "Cynefin 101 – Portfolio Management." *InfoQ*. C4Media Inc, 26 Dec. 2014. Web. 20 May 2015.

Brougham, Greg. "Cynefin 101 – Shared Context and Sense Making." *InfoQ*. C4Media Inc, 4 Apr. 2015. Web. 19 May 2015.

Carey, Benedict. "Learning to See Data." *The New York Times*. The New York Times Company, 28 Mar. 2015. Web. 15 May 2015.

Covert, Abby, and Nicole Fenton. *How to Make Sense of Any Mess*. N.p.: CreateSpace Independent Platform, 2014.

Church, Matt, Peter Cook, and Scott Stein. *Sell Your Thoughts: How to Earn a Million Dollars a Year as a Thought Leader*. Auckland, N.Z.: HarperCollins, 2011.

Dervin, Brenda. "Sense-making Theory and Practice: An Overview of User Interests in Knowledge Seeking and Use." *J of Knowledge Management Journal of Knowledge Management* 2.2 (1998): 36-46. Web.

Dervin, Brenda. "Chaos, Order and Sense Making: A Proposed Theory for Information Design." Ed. Robert Jacobson. *Information Design* (1999): 35-57.

Garreau, Lionel, Philippe Mouricou, and Amaury Grimand. "Drawing on the Map: An Exploration of Strategic Sensemaking/Giving Practices Using Visual Representations." *British Journal of Management* 00 (2015): 1-24. *Readcube*. Labtiva Inc, 2015. Web. 20 May 2015.

Gorsht, Reuven. "Are You Ready? Here Are The Top 10 Skills For The Future." *Forbes*. Forbes Magazine, 12 May 2014. Web. 20 May 2015.

Haudan, Jim. *The Art of Engagement Bridging the Gap Between People and Possibilities*. N.p.: McGraw-Hill, 2008. Electronic.

Hewitt-Gleeson, Michael. *English Thinking: The Three Methods*. N.p.: School of Thinking, 2012. Electronic.

Holzmer, David. "Our Un-killable Mechanistic Thinking Warps Organizations' Awareness of Human Behavior." Weblog post. *GonnaGrowWings*. N.p., 07 Jan. 2015. Web. 20 May 2015.

Holzmer, David. "The Collapse of Expertise and Rise of Collaborative Sensemaking." Weblog post. *GonnaGrowWings*. N.p., 11 Mar. 2015. Web. 20 May 2015.

Hurson, Tim. *Think Better: (your Company's Future Depends on It ... and so Does Yours)*. New York: McGraw-Hill, 2008. Electronic.

Jones, Peter. "Sensemaking Methodology: A Liberation Theory of Communicative Agency." Weblog post. *EPIC*. N.p., 6 Apr. 2015. Web. 20 May 2015.

Kahneman, Daniel. *Thinking, Fast and Slow*. New York: Farrar, Straus and Giroux, 2011.

"Karl E. Weick." - Wikiquote. N.p., 2 Nov. 2014. Web. 20 May 2015.

Klein, Gary. *Seeing What Others Don't: The Remarkable Ways We Gain Insights*. New York: PublicAffairs, 2013. Electronic.

Kolko, Jon. "Abductive Thinking and Sensemaking: The Drivers of Design Synthesis." *MIT's Design Issues* Winter 2010 26.1 (2010): n. pag. *Jon Kolko*. Web. 20 May 2015.

Kolko, Jon. "Sensemaking and Framing: A Theoretical Reflection on Perspective in Design Synthesis." *Jon Kolko*. Proc. of Design Research Society Conference. N.p., 2010. Web. 19 May 2015.

Landry, Bridget. "Hot Off the Presses: Healthcare Narrative Playbook!" Weblog post. *Business Innovation Factory*. N.p., 7 Apr. 2015. Web. 20 May 2015.

LeFever, Lee. *The Art of Explanation: Making Your Ideas, Products and Services Easier to Understand*. Hoboken, NJ: John Wiley & Sons, 2013. Electronic.

Madsbjerg, Christian, and Mikkel Rasmussen. "An Anthropologist Walks into a Bar..." *Harvard Business Review*. Harvard Business School Publishing, Mar. 2014. Web. 15 May 2015.

Madsbjerg, Christian, and Mikkel B. Rasmussen. *The Moment of Clarity: Using the Human Sciences to Solve Your Toughest Business Problems*. Boston: Harvard Business Review Press, 2014.

Maitlis, Sally, and Marlys Christianson. "Sensemaking In Organizations: Taking Stock And Moving Forward." *The Academy of Management Annals* (2013): 1-98.

Markman, Arthur B. *Smart Thinking: Three Essential Keys to Solve Problems, Innovate, and Get Things Done*. New York: Perigee, 2012.

Ogden, Curtis. "Networks, Collective Impact and the Place of Expertise." Weblog post. *Interaction Institute for Social Change*. N.p., 08 Apr. 2015. Web. 20 May 2015.

Pastor, Elizabeth. "Using Information Visualization to Prepare for ChangeMaking." Game Changers. California, San Francisco. 11 Nov. 2012. *Issuu*. Web. 19 May 2015.

Popova, Maria. "100 Diagrams That Changed the World." *Brain Pickings RSS*. N.p., n.d. Web. 19 May 2015.

Rasmussen, Mikkel. "Lego's Serious Play." Weblog post. *Strategy+business*. PwC Strategy & LLC, 26 Mar. 2015. Web. 20 May 2015.

Rixon, Andrew. "Great Quote from Brian Arthur on Sensemaking." Weblog post. *Anecdote*. N.p., 16 Oct. 2005. Web. 19 May 2015.

Rosline, Abdul Kadir, and Norzanah Mat Nor. *Managing Knowledge Workers in a Knowledge-based Economy: The Changing Role of Human Resource Management in the MSC Status Companies, Malaysia*. Thesis. Cardiff University, 2005. Wales, UK: HRM Department, Cardiff Business School, 2005.

Savolainen, Reijo. "Information Use as Gap-bridging: The Viewpoint of Sense-making Methodology." *J. Am. Soc. Inf. Sci. Journal of the American Society for Information Science and Technology* 57.8 (2006): 1116-125. 25 Apr. 2006. Web.

Senge, Peter M. *The Fifth Discipline: The Art and Practice of the Learning Organization*. New York: Doubleday/Currency, 1990.

Siemens, George. "What I've Learned in My First Week of a Dual-layer MOOC (DALMOOC)." Weblog post. *Elearnspace*. N.p., 28 Oct. 2014. Web. 19 May 2015.

Snook, Scott A. *The Handbook for Teaching Leadership: Knowing, Doing, and Being*. Thousand Oaks: SAGE Publications, 2012.

Sobel-Lojeski, Karen. "The Subtle Ways Our Screens Are Pushing Us Apart." *Harvard Business Review*. Harvard Business School Publishing, 08 Apr. 2015. Web. 20 May 2015.

The Institute for the Future for the University of Phoenix Research Institute, *Future Work Skills2020 Report*, Palo Alto CA, www.iftf.org

Van Dijk, Menno, and Berend-Jan Hilberts. "Sensing Is Exploring Uncharted Territory." *THNK. School of Creative Leadership*. N.p., 16 Apr. 2014. Web. 20 May 2015.

Weick, Karl E. *Sensemaking in Organizations*. Thousand Oaks: Sage Publications, 1995.

Wrzesniewski, Amy, Jane E. Dutton, and Gelaye Debebe. "Interpersonal Sensemaking and The Meaning of Work." *Research in Organizational Behavior* 25 (2003): 95-135. *Michigan Ross*. Web. 15 May 2015.

"People in business want the same thing—the chance to play in a real game where everyone can show what they can do to contribute to a victory."

From The Art of Engagement: Bridging the Gap Between
People and Possibilities

- Jim Haudan

About the Author - Lynne Cazaly

Lynne Cazaly is a keynote speaker, author and adviser. She is the author of the books:

- *Create Change: How to apply innovation in an era of uncertainty, and*
- *Visual Mojo: How to capture thinking, convey information and collaborate using visuals*
- *Do-Doos: The shit that gets in the way of doing good work*

She works with executives, senior leaders and teams on major change and transformation projects. She helps people distil their thinking, apply ideas and innovation and boost the engagement and collaboration effectiveness of teams.

Lynne assists organizations with creative and engaging facilitated workshops, skills development in creative and innovative thinking and she works with people to help them unlock the 'entrepreneur inside'.

Lynne is an experienced board director and chair and is a global keynote speaker and an executive facilitator. She is on the faculty of Thought Leaders Business School.

Find out more at www.lynnecazaly.com
email her at info@lynnecazaly.com
or find her on Twitter at @lynnecazaly

Other Books by the Author

Create Change: How to apply innovation in an era of uncertainty

When leaders need to lead teams through change, it's vital they create an environment that brings people along ... to leverage the transformation, rather than blocking or fighting it

To boost competitive advantage, career success and team performance, it's all about how well you can 'create change.' Create Change is about: having a spirit of spontaneity, experimenting , co-creating and having an intrepid curiosity.

Together the capabilities, techniques and approaches outlined in 'Create Change' will help you lead through change, leverage it and ... even like it.

Author and leadership communications expert Lynne Cazaly gives you the capabilities and thinking to strengthen your ability to respond, adapt and lead teams through change and transformation.Building on the success of Lynne's first book 'Visual Mojo', 'Create Change' takes engagement, communication and collaboration further. Packed with tips, advice, insights and tried and tested creative lessons, Create Change will show you how to:

- lead change
- think critically
- apply innovation

Great leadership communicators aren't born; they are made. Whether you are leading a team through change or are on the receiving end of a corporate transformation, this book will help you think and act creatively to make change a process you welcome, thrive in and leverage for stellar performance.

Making Sense - Lynne Cazaly

Other Books by the Author

Visual Mojo: How to capture thinking, convey information and collaborate using visuals

This is not a book you sit down and read. This is a book I want you to write and draw in! With 168 pages of reading, learning, examples and space to sketch!

Now you can learn the powerful techniques of sketching, scribing and visualizing, includes 60 icons, space to practice and suggestions for their meaning, use and application

This book is a workshop in your hands, an opportunity for you to get more out of your brain and get your visual mojo back.

This book is about moving you from being someone who talks about their thinking and ideas … to someone who captures and conveys that thinking and achieves greater engagement, buy-in and influence doing that.

This book will enable you to:

- start using visuals in your brainstorming and ideation
- capture key points from workshops, meetings and discussions
- map out conversations and thinking
- boost your confidence and get over the 'I can't draw' syndrome
- build your visual dictionary of icons, symbols and visuals to use.

⭐ www.lynnecazaly·com